So Your Child Can't Read

What's Next?

Veronica Jennings McCarthy M.Ed

GabrielPress

For more information please visit: www.TheReadingTutor.org

GabrielPress: www.GabrielPressUSA.com

Chicago, Ill. 60655

The author and publisher have taken reasonable precautions in the preparation of this book and believe the information presented in the book is accurate as of the date it was written. However, neither the author nor the publisher assumes any responsibility for any errors or omissions. The author and publisher specifically disclaim any liability resulting from the use or application of the information contained in this book, and the information in not intended to serve as legal, financial or other professional advice related to individual situations. The views and opinions herein are solely the author's.

ISBN Number: 978-0-9835597-1-9

Printed and bound in the United States of America

To Jesus, Mary and Joseph,
the source of all inspiration and courage.

In loving memory of my father,
Richard D. Jennings,
who is dearly missed.

To Kathy, who said I could.
To Caitlin, who inspired the journey.

Optimum Nutrition and Learning

Optimal nutrition plays a key role in optimal learning. Current food trends can make it extremely difficult, if not impossible, to get optimal nutrition from food alone. This can have a detrimental effect on learning, especially with individuals with a learning difference. I personally know that finding a high quality nutritional product can be a daunting task. With this in mind, I wholeheartedly recommend and market a patented nutritional product that my family has been using for ten years. We have had phenomenal results. For more information please visit: www.TheReadingTutor.org and click on Optimal Nutrition.

Before we begin...

Points to Ponder

- Your child has great gifts and unlimited potential.

- Your child **can** and **will** learn how to read with your help.

- Your attitude will affect your child's attitude. Your perception of any situation will be a huge determining factor in your outcome. Having a positive perception and attitude definitely increase your success.

- Your child's self-esteem is most certainly adversely affected if he/ she is struggling with learning to read. You will need to take measures to boost his/ her self-esteem.

- Reward systems motivate. Positive reinforcement motivates.

- What a person believes to be true becomes his reality. A child who believes he is unsuccessful will become unsuccessful. But, change that belief and you will change that result. "Change your thoughts and you change your destiny." In the big scheme of things, a reading difference is not a major issue, unless it goes unaddressed. Then it becomes a major influencing issue in a person's life.

- A reading disability is **NOT** a lack of intelligence. It is a **learning difference**. We need to discover how each individual child learns best and then provide this learning platform for him/her.

"To become convinced that you can succeed is the first requisite to success."

Wallace D. Wattles

Table of Contents

Introduction

"Whatever the mind of man can conceive, and believe, it can achieve"

Napolean Hill

So your child can't read. What's next? There are three facts you should know upfront.

1. Your child is not the only one having trouble learning to read.
2. Your child is NOT stupid.
3. This can be an asset.

Your Child is Not Alone

First of all, you should know that your child is not alone. This is a very common problem. According to statistics, at least one third of all children in any given school will have some degree of difficulty learning to read the traditional way.

Your child could also be dyslexic. Dyslexia is not uncommon and tends to run in families. A few sites to begin your search into dyslexia are: www.ncld.org; www.ncbi-nlm.nih.gov; www.interdys.org. Your child could also have one of a myriad of different types of learning disabilities or was born with some condition that is impacting his learning.

This will not change the fact that your child can be successful in learning how to <u>read</u>. Each child is unique and will learn according to the genetic make-up of his brain, learning style, learning strengths and weaknesses.

The length of time needed for your child to complete a program and improve his reading abilities will vary according to your child's own personal needs and abilities. An exact time line cannot be put on learning to read because of the enormous differences in children. If your child is having trouble learning to read, this book can guide you in determining the solution.

A Reading Difficulty Does Not Mean Low Intelligence

Second, having trouble learning to read does NOT mean that your child has a lower level of intelligence. Often the opposite is true and your child is not only very intelligent but blessed with a brain that is "wired" to learn differently. Do not think of your child as having a learning disability. Instead, think of your child as a unique learner with many hidden talents waiting to be uncovered.

The following list of famous people who struggled with reading should help you and your child to know that you are in great company: Albert Einstein, George Washington, Steve Jobs, Thomas Edison, John F. Kennedy, Nelson Rockefeller, Hans Christian Anderson, Alexander Graham Bell, Sir Winston Churchill, Leonardo da Vinci, Henry Ford, and Thomas Jefferson, (just to name a few.) Not only did all these people struggle with reading they also all had significant people in their lives that encouraged them and prompted them to keep going until they were successful.

A Learning Difference Can be an Asset

Finally, this can actually be an asset. The brain that thinks "outside the box" will look at problems differently and reach novel solutions. All of the famous people listed above did just that and were well known for their unique thinking skills.

An MRI can show which area of the brain is activated during the reading process. A brain that can read easily will activate a different area of the brain than the brain that finds reading difficult. You can train your child's brain to actually make new pathways into different areas of the brain and become a better reader. One way to achieve this is through multisensory learning methods. This will be discussed more in depth in later chapters.

A struggling reader feels stupid (to put it bluntly). They see their classmates learning to read easily and think something is wrong with them because they cannot do it. A common mistake before a child is diagnosed is the misconception that the child is not working hard enough or that the child is lazy. Often, the child is working much harder than his peers, but is not "getting it."

Sometimes a child is held back a year in school to give him time to catch up to his peers. Then he is taught using the same methods which were not successful the first time. These methods are not successful again. Now he is a "double" failure. This will definitely cause self-esteem issues and probably a lot of trouble at home as well as in school.

A Reading Difficulty Can Permeate All Areas of a Person's Life

A reading difficulty does not just stop at poor grades. It infiltrates into every other aspect of a child's life and can drag down the child's ultimate potential. This is preventable with the appropriate instruction at the appropriate time. Everyone should have the ability to enjoy a good book. Everyone should have the ability to learn from a book. Not achieving this ability is a crime in this day and age. But this is exactly what we do when a child in our care (parent or teacher) does not learn how to read fluently.

Self-Esteem

Another crucial concern at this point is the child's self-esteem. Parents and teachers have to continuously highlight the child's strengths, gifts and abilities in order to keep his self-esteem at a high level. Some children can give up on themselves during this time which can manifest in a lot of different ways, predominately negative. A child may begin acting out in class, fighting about doing homework, refusing to read at home, or even refusing to go to school. This is normal and understandable. School is hard. Reading is hard. The child does not feel like he fits in anymore. It is very important for both you and your child to keep your attitudes very positive towards any aspect of school or reading during this time.

Positive Reinforcement Works Best

Do not punish by taking away games or privileges. You do not want to make this situation any more heated than it might be already. You need to put in place a rewards program that works for both of you which I will discuss more in depth in a later chapter. This will bring a more positive approach to the situation. Your child is going to have to work very hard to develop reading skills and I believe he should be compensated for this extra effort. This will also motivate him to work even harder, which is what we want. You would expect extra compensation at work if you put in more effort and hours than your job description called for, so why not give your child the same compensation.

Intrinsic motivation is fine for an adult, but you cannot expect a child to put in long hours of very difficult brain work just so he will feel better about himself. Not at this early age and not in the beginning of a new reading intervention. We can teach intrinsic motivation along the way but for now let us just reward him for working extra hard. As a child begins to see progress and become more confident in his abilities, he will begin to approach reading with less trepidation and eventually find reading enjoyable. This is our goal.

My Philosophy on Reading

Before I go any farther, I should share how I developed my philosophy on reading instruction. I graduated with a BS Degree in Mathematics Education. Initially I wanted to teach Mathematics but my interests changed after I witnessed firsthand the far reaching and highly debilitating effects a reading disability can have on a child. I had no idea that learning to read could be a problem. I learned to read easily when I was a child and my first daughter seemed to learn how to read on her own. I thought that children just automatically learned how to read during kindergarten.

Then came my second daughter. No matter what we did, she could not learn the alphabet. She could not sing the alphabet song or learn the sight words she was supposed to know in kindergarten. After a lot of pain, fighting, crying and two years of torture in kindergarten, and a heart breaking unsuccessful two years in first and second grade, we uncovered the fact that she had dyslexia as well as a severe Central Auditory Processing Disability (CAPD). During this time I read every book on reading that I could find. I went on to acquire a Master's Degree in Reading and became a Reading Specialist.

I taught for many years in the public and private school system as a reading specialist and tutored privately one-on-one. I worked with children that had many different physical disabilities as well as learning disabilities. I have been over the road of reading difficulties as a parent and as a reading specialist. I know how you feel as a parent because I already felt all the emotions and fears that go along with this territory. I know what to do as a teacher because I have studied and taught all aspects of reading acquisition for over 20 years. I developed Reading Blocks: A Step by Step Method to Teach Reading during this period. This all came about in my quest to find the solution to my daughter's inability to learn how to read.

My philosophy on literacy education lies in the belief that every child has the right and the ability to learn how to read. This can be accomplished with:

- highly trained teachers
- informed instruction based on current research
- tier leveled instruction and intervention where necessary
- instructional strategies based on students' culture, background and interests

The Matthew Effect

A quality education is necessary for the future success of our children and this cannot be accomplished without effective reading skills. According to Dr. Stanovich's theory, known as the Matthew Effect, children need to leave the second grade as accomplished readers or risk spending their academic careers at the bottom of the class. This finding can be very frightening to a parent with a child who cannot read. Dr. Stanovich's work confirmed what I witnessed first-hand with my daughter; sufficient reading ability is crucial to a child's future success in life.

Children need to acquire reading skills and confidence in their reading ability, during kindergarten and first grade. The lack of either will have an exponential negative growth impact over the years. According to the Matthew Effect, students who read frequently acquire greater growth in reading skills, vocabulary, and basic knowledge while students who read infrequently, due to lack of skills or lack of confidence, fall farther and farther behind. "The rich get richer and the poor get poorer," according to Dr. Stanovich. By third grade, a struggling reader has a very slim chance of catching up to his peers in reading ability, vocabulary and basic knowledge, without intensive intervention. Current reading research spotlights the importance of identifying at risk students before a reading problem develops. The ill effects of a reading difficulty can change a life and last a lifetime. Intervention at an early age is crucial.

Parents' Responsibility

School districts will vary enormously in the reading programs they offer. Some school districts are better equipped to handle the reading difficulties of their students. Lack of funds in a district can result in less programs being offered and less personnel to work with the students.

Parents need to be aware of the reading programs offered in their school district and to seek outside sources when the school cannot offer what their child needs. This predominately is not the fault of the teachers or the schools but usually a lack of funds.

Sometimes parents are tempted to deny any need on their part to rectify their child's reading disability with the notion that this is the schools' responsibility. This is definitely the wrong attitude and will only hurt the child. Ultimately, making sure that a child learns how to read in the early grades is the responsibility of the parent. No one loves your child more than you. No one wants your child to be successful more than you. It is up to you as the parent to make sure your child receives the instruction or intervention he needs. Sometimes that means paying more money out of pocket or putting in more one on one time, or getting what your child needs outside of the school district. This is a small price to pay in the big picture for your child's success. Your child has a future job to do and one very important step in this preparation is learning how to read fluently.

Appropriate Intervention

Reading research shows the effectiveness of **appropriate** intervention in helping struggling readers. Just as all students are not the same, all interventions should not be the same. A reading intervention program must be matched to a student's reading needs like a puzzle piece fitting into another puzzle piece. Anything less than a perfect fit is detrimental to a student's timely acquisition of reading skills. A student with more reading needs should receive a greater amount of reading intervention time, in addition to the regular classroom reading instruction. I strongly believe that all children are not only capable of <u>learning</u> to read but <u>loving</u> to read.

There is a multitudinous amount of reading intervention programs, and reading materials available today. Some are great, some are not so great, and some are actually detrimental to a struggling reader's progress. The job of sifting through all this information can be a daunting task for a parent or a new teacher looking for material or a program to use with a struggling reader.

In later chapters, I recommend several professional programs that I have researched and used over the years. I found these programs to be extremely effective in teaching a struggling learner how to read. If cost is an issue, a parent can choose to teach their child how to read at home. With this need in mind, I developed a program for parents to use at home to teach their child how to read.

Reading Blocks: A Step by Step Method to Teach Reading (the second book in the Reading Tutor Series) contains a complete system to teach a child to read using inexpensive materials which you can make yourself. My goal is to make teaching reading accessible to anyone with a desire to do so. This book is appropriate for: a parent wanting to teach their child to read; anyone with a dream to begin a reading tutoring business from home; a teacher looking for ideas to improve a reading program or reach a struggling student; a school looking for a cost effective means to improve their students' reading scores by incorporating the help of parents trained with this resource.

Summary of Chapters

Hopefully, you now feel better about your child's situation and you are motivated to begin the process. What do you do next?

Your first job as a parent of a struggling reader is to continuously build-up your child's self-esteem during this time. Chapter 1 discusses this topic as well as how to implement a system for positive reinforcement. Positive reinforcement is one key for opening the door of success. Learning to read can be extremely difficult for some kids and positive reinforcement gives them the incentive to continue to work hard.

Next, you need to know what is involved in learning to read. Chapter 2 discusses the process of learning to read. This will help you to understand what your child needs to know and why. This chapter will also give you the tools to discern if the program you have chosen for your child is actually working.

Your next job is to collect information about your child. Chapter 3 discusses what you need to know and how to go about obtaining this information. A successful reading program will begin on the current reading level of your child and then will follow a detailed map for where he needs to go.

After collecting all the data pertaining to your child's skills, you will need to sit down with a team of professionals and discuss all this information. Usually this occurs in an IEP (Individualized Education Program) meeting. Chapter 4 discusses what to expect in an IEP meeting and how you can participate to obtain the best results for your child.

Once you have all the information, and discussed the situation with professionals, you will need to make a decision about your child's reading education. You will hear recommendations from the IEP team but the final decision is yours. Chapter 5 discusses the choices you have concerning your child's reading program. After reading this chapter, you will make a decision on the program that best suits your child's unique situation.

The focus of Chapters 6, 7, and 8 is to help you implement the program you choose, as well as evaluate the program as you progress. Each chapter will discuss implementing and evaluating either the school program, private program, or at-home program. Each chapter will also identify warning flags to look for in a program that is not working. This will help you to monitor your child's success, or lack of success, no matter which program you choose.

Chapter 9 presents stories of several children who struggled with reading and how they became fluent readers. Each child has their own set of unique gifts and challenges and some of the learning issues involved include: autism, dyslexia, parental drug use, birth defects, children for whom English is a second language, and more.

The personal stories will help you to see that you and your child are not alone in the struggle of learning to read. Millions of people have gone through this struggle before you and millions of others will follow you.

Chapters 10 and 11 discuss a detailed description of each recommended reading program. Chapter 10 discusses professional programs and Chapter 11 discusses at-home programs.

Chapter 12 discusses several multisensory activities to use which will greatly enhance learning and remembering components in the reading process.

So now, brace yourself, and get ready to begin the long trek out of the frustrating world of a struggling reader. You can do this successfully! Your child can do this successfully! On both accounts I am certain.

Points to Ponder

- Your child has great gifts and unlimited potential.
- Your child **can** and **will** learn how to read with your help.
- Your attitude will affect your child's attitude. **Positive-Positive-Positive**
- Your child's self-esteem is most certainly adversely affected. You will need to boost it.
- Reward systems motivate. Positive reinforcement motivates.

Chapter 1

Building Self-Esteem and Motivation

"Change your thoughts and you change your destiny"

Dr. Joseph Murphy

Positive Self-Esteem is Crucial to Success

This section is in the beginning of the book because it is one of the most crucial components for the success of any reading program. The results in any reading program will be lacking without a willing participant. The child has to believe completely that he can be successful or he will not be successful. The child has to be highly motivated to do his best or he will not do his best. Period. The issues of self-esteem and motivation need to be tackled first for the greatest level of success in any reading program.

These components can be easy or difficult to address depending on the age of the child and how long he has gone without being diagnosed. The self-esteem issue is easiest to address when you discover the learning difference early, for example in kindergarten or preschool. Usually a younger child is eager to learn and has an open opinion about his ability to learn. So when you catch this issue early he is game for anything. A child in this situation will usually also be easy to motivate and very willing to work hard in a reading program.

An older child, on the other hand, who has struggled with reading for a couple of years, or maybe even several years, will very likely have an extremely jilted opinion about his abilities regarding reading. He probably also has a strong aversion to anything involving reading.

Perhaps, kids at school might have made fun of him. Teachers may have been lacking in either recognizing the issue or knowledge of what to do about the issue, or maybe just had poor dispositions. Just be aware that there may be a variety of negative experiences which your child has not shared with you but which are feeding into his poor attitude or low self-esteem. This type of situation will be more difficult to rectify, but again it depends on the child's personality and his unique situation. Whether your child is easy to motivate and has a high self-esteem or not is just a matter of degree, both scenarios can be successful.

First and most important, your child must **KNOW** he is smart and capable of doing anything he chooses to do. He must **KNOW** it, not think it. This is important. A child who knows he is smart will accomplish a whole lot more than a child who thinks he is a loser or incapable of doing anything. There have been many studies done to prove this idea to be true.

Performance Matches Expectations

An experiment carried out in a school setting backed this assumption. The school called a group of teachers into a conference with the principal before the school year began. The person doing the experiment told the teachers that they were chosen to participate in this study because their past performance proved that they were the highest performing teachers in the school district. They were told this quality was needed for the success of this experiment.

Next, they were told they were going to receive the highest performing children in the district. They were also told that the administration of the district expected their classrooms to outperform every other classroom in the district since the highest performing teachers were teaching the students with the highest IQs.

As expected, these classrooms performed better than any of the other classrooms in the districts. At the end of the year, the teachers were again called into a conference. They were told that they performed better than any of the classrooms that were not a part of this study. They were also told that they were really chosen for this experiment randomly. Their names were pulled out of a hat filled with the names of every teacher in the district. The children in their classrooms were also chosen randomly from every child in the district. The only reason their classrooms achieved this level of success was because the teachers and the students **knew** that they were the best. They **expected** themselves to achieve the highest levels.

The teacher's and student's approach to all obstacles during the year was based on the knowledge that they were the highest performing teachers and students in the district. They believed this to be true so they acted in this manner. They knew this to be true because the leaders in their district told them it was true. Nothing else mattered, except the fact that they knew they were the best. **Their performance matched their expectation**.

Performance Matches Expectations in the Home

A second example of this paradigm is from Napolean Hill, the author of *Think and Grow Rich*. His son was born without ears. He had no known apparatus for hearing. Hill was told that his son had a disability and should attend a special school for children with disabilities and also learn sign language to communicate. Napolean Hill refused to believe that his son had a disability. He refused to allow his son, or anyone in his family for that matter, to believe that the boy had a disability. He said he strongly believed that for every challenge a person encountered in his life, there was an equal level of opportunity waiting to be exposed. He applied this belief to his sons' situation.

Napolean Hill could have just listened to the "experts" and placed his son in special education. He could have lowered any expectations he had for his child compared to the expectations he had for his "normal" children. But he did not. He fought the school district every year to have this child in a regular classroom. Every day he informed his son that not having ears held great blessings for him. He also prepared his son to expect great things from having this "advantage." He did not say "disadvantage." His son did go on to live a very successful and fruitful life and his "disability" was in fact the key to his success. This was a direct result of the beliefs his father imbued in him from his birth. **His performance matched his expectation**.

What a person believes to be true becomes his reality. A child who believes he is unsuccessful will become unsuccessful. But, change that belief and you will change that result. "Change your thoughts and you change your destiny". In the big scheme of things, a reading difference is not a major issue, unless it goes unaddressed. Then it becomes a major influencing issue in a person's life.

One of the most important roles we have as parents is to support and encourage our children to reach their full potential, whatever level that may be. Parents need to continuously envelop their children with the understanding and belief that they are smart and capable and will accomplish great things. Hold the expectation yourself, and then transfer that expectation to your child. Continuously show your child that this is true by pointing out little things they do daily that prove this to be true.

For example, you can point out to your child his amazing ability to tie shoelaces. You can inform him that he must be so smart because he tied his shoelaces earlier and better than anyone else. Or you can tell him that he is the best skater, or singer, or whatever skill that best applies to your child. The accomplishment does not have to be something big and important. You just make it big and important. Your child looks up to you and believes you. You can build him up in a thousand different ways every day. These little things will make a big improvement in your child's self-esteem and consequently in all areas of your child's life. Just remember, his performance will match his expectation. You need to build up and reinforce that expectation.

I know that if we give the idea of the performance matching the expectation more attention, in every area of our lives, we will surpass all of our previous achievements. We need to definitely attach this idea to our children with learning differences. Come to think of it, why do we call it a "reading disability"? It really is only a "difference" from the average way of learning, but not necessarily a disability. It is only a disability when we believe it is a disability and call it one. Now, let us apply this idea to the child who is having trouble learning to read.

Transfer Positive Mental Attitude to Child

You should call your child into a conference and tell him that you know he is smart. You have always recognized how smart and capable he was and is. Point out everything he is good at no matter how small the ability might seem to you. You want to make him feel good about himself and some accomplishments he has made so far in his life.

After acknowledging all that he is good at, approach the reading difficulty. Explain to him that you can see that he is having trouble learning to read and that just means that he learns differently. Help him to understand that this is an asset. His brain is "wired" differently so he will learn differently.

This gift will also enable him to access different areas of his brain and reach different levels of knowledge that "average" people cannot reach. This is true. NASA hires a higher percentage of employees with dyslexia than without dyslexia. They look for this trait. They recognize this "disability" as a coveted asset. Your child must understand this and believe this also.

The positive mental attitude you bring to the table when dealing with the reading issue will make all the difference in the outcome. You want to transfer your positive mental attitude to your child. This means you need to cultivate one if you do not have one already.

Now that you discussed how smart your child is and how learning differently is an asset, you have prepared him mentally to approach the task of learning to read with a positive attitude. The next step to address is motivation.

Motivation

How do we motivate a child to work extra hard at something that is extremely difficult for him? The best way to motivate a child is with positive reinforcement techniques. We reward him, not punish him. We focus on positive behavior, not negative. We give something that is desired, not take something away .

Let us pretend that you have a job with a boss who gives you a very difficult assignment. You are working as hard as you can to complete this assignment but it is very difficult for you and you have to put in a lot of overtime. Even though you are working your hardest, your boss calls you into his office and berates you, and ridicules you, and calls you lazy because you still have not finished this simple assignment. You know that you are working your hardest and putting in long hours. How do you feel?

In this situation, you probably feel like quitting. You definitely do not feel like working extremely hard for a person who treats you this way. You might even think that since he does not appreciate the amount of hard work and effort you have put forth so far, why bother working this hard. You are not receiving any recognition for your effort, not to mind overtime pay, so why bother. You might decide to either discontinue putting forth all that effort or even quit the job completely.

I believe our delayed readers often times feel this way. They are working so hard to learn how to read, and it is extremely difficult for them, but no one is acknowledging or recognizing this fact. And to make matters worse, their friends all learn effortlessly, while they struggle with the basics, regardless of how much effort they put forth. On top of all this, they might even be called stupid or lazy by someone they respect, when actually the exact opposite is true.

Now what if that same boss called you in and said how grateful he was for your hard work. How he noticed all the overtime you were putting in, and he really appreciated your effort. What if he said that he knew you were the only one who could complete this project and that is why he chose you out of the whole staff? What if he also even gave you a bonus or a raise? How would you feel then?

You would probably redouble your efforts to complete the project no matter what effort it took on your part. Your boss knew you could do it, so you would do it. Your boss appreciated your efforts and rewarded you with praise and a bonus or raise, which in turn motivated you to do your best.

This is exactly what we need to do for our children who have trouble learning to read. We need to praise them for all their hard work and encourage them to continue working hard. We need to acknowledge the effort they are putting forth and reward them for all the extra effort they need to put forth. We need to continuously remind them of how smart they are because they are not going to feel smart at this time. This positive attitude will accomplish so much more, and in a shorter amount of time, than all the negative behaviors and attitudes. Plant the thought in your child that he is good and smart and capable, and these are the qualities that will develop and strengthen and grow. And rewarding him a little something does not hurt either.

Positive Reinforcement

This leads me to positive reinforcement techniques. How can you positively reinforce your child's efforts in a way that will make him work extra hard for an extended period of time? This is easy. Reward him. What does your child love to do? Think of whatever he loves and plan a reward system around this object or activity.

For example, if a child loves horses then plan several rewards around a horse theme. Have a chart for every day of the week. Decide how much the child has to accomplish to earn a sticker for the chart. After he completes the work he puts the sticker on the chart. When he gets a certain amount of stickers, he earns the reward. You might decide that for every 5 stickers he can have a horseback riding lesson. Or maybe when he completes up to a certain point in a reading program, he can attend a summer camp with horses.

The reward should be extremely personal. The child needs to pick it out and really want it for this to be a motivating force. You both need to sit down together and work out what the reward is and how much it "costs". Costs meaning how much effort your child will have to put forth to achieve this reward. Usually this entails some bargaining and compromising on both sides. Eventually, you should be able to reach an end result which works for both of you.

Remember, you want the end result to motivate your child. So it is in your best interest to be flexible during negotiations if this result will be seen by your child as something extremely worthwhile or desirable.

A younger child is much easier to motivate. A treasure chest filled with small toys and candy always works well. Each prize in the treasure chest should have a sticker with a "price." The child can receive a ticket for each reading session where he worked hard. Extra tickets can be given for extra work. The tickets can then be used to "buy" a prize from the treasure chest.

I used this both in a school setting and at home with my own children. It worked equally well in both situations. In the school, I held a "shopping" day once a week so it would not take up too much time. Whenever I purchased more prizes for the chest, I spread them out on a table so everyone could see what was available. They were given time to look it all over and decide what they wanted to "buy." This gave every child motivation to work hard for me and cost me very little. Friday was our shopping day in the school setting. The children knew that I would give them time every Friday to purchase their prizes. If they wanted a certain item that cost more than they could "afford", I would hold the item for them until they saved enough tickets. They always worked extra hard when there was a coveted item waiting for them.

I also used this at home for my daughters. I would fill the chest with items I knew they wanted. They would redeem their tickets whenever they had enough tickets to pay for it. I knew I had the right items in the chest when the child would ask me to do a reading lesson instead of me reminding her.

You know your child best. Choose a reward or prize that is best suited to him. If it is something like horseback riding lessons, cut up a picture of a horse, and post it in a prominent spot. Each time he completes whatever task you both previously agreed upon (maybe one lesson or one week of lessons), he can put one piece of the horse on the refrigerator. He earns the lessons when the whole horse is completed. You can do this with anything the child wants to earn. A visual helps to keep him motivated if it is a long term goal while tickets work well for short and long term goals.

This type of positive reinforcement makes the added work load more doable for a child, and as a consequence, more doable for you. The reward system makes working hard a little more fun. Just make sure you continue the verbal praise also. That is still the most crucial aspect of positive reinforcement.

Points to Ponder

- The child must **know** he is smart and capable of accomplishing great things.
- Performance matches Expectations
- A learning difference is **NOT** a disability, and usually disguises great gifts.
- A positive mental attitude in parent and child is crucial for success.
- Rewards work.

Chapter 2

Introduction to the Reading Process

"Our only limitations are those we set up on our own minds."

Napolean Hill

Research has shown that the most effective way to teach reading is with a program that is:

- research based
- directly taught in a sequential and cumulative manner
- uses multisensory techniques
- phonics based

In other words, the program should be taught in identifiable chunks, according to a definite map of what chunks to know at what time, and in what order, and it should use a specific learning technique.

Each new progression in a cumulative program builds on the previous chunk of knowledge. A child's progression in reading halts when he tries to build upon a base that is missing information or has faulty information. His façade of learning collapses at this point. This is when many children start memorizing. They memorize as many words as they can by the shape of the word or by using the first sound to guess at the word. They can fool people for a while with this strategy because kindergarten and the beginning of first grade have a limited range of words. Eventually, the child falls farther and farther behind and accumulates a larger and larger store of erroneous information that has to be uncovered and unlearned.

Why Memorizing Fails

During testing of a group of First graders, I had a child read a First grade book perfectly to me. When I asked her to turn to the last page and read the words backwards, she could not read a single word. She had memorized this book as well as many other books, but could not decode the words.

Obviously, memorizing all the books is not possible and this child was falling behind her peers and becoming increasingly frustrated with the whole reading process. In her mind, reading was memorizing. On closer inspection, I discovered that she did not know many of the sounds of the letters and could not blend or segment sounds. Since this was uncovered early, I was able to work with her one on one and she was reading at grade level in a couple of months.

The important point to note is that a struggling reader learns to compensate and blend in with the other children. They have a myriad of strategies to keep under the radar of the teacher and also keep themselves from looking different. The longer it goes uncovered, the longer it takes to remedy.

Many schools have programs in place to catch these struggling readers early. The best time to find out a child has a reading difficulty is during preschool or kindergarten. Then you can catch them before they fall behind. Remember, the Matthew Effect states that if they are not fluent readers by the end of second grade, they run the risk of continuing to lag behind their peers in increasingly large increments. This can have a negative impact on the whole range of their learning.

Reading Failure Has Devastating Effects

Each grade above second grade without efficient reading skills will have an exponential negative effect on the child's learning. Why limit anyone in this manner. A reading difference can be and should be discovered and addressed at a young age for the quickest resolution.

The greater the discrepancy between where a child's reading skills are and where the reading skills should be, and the grade level, the greater the length of time it takes to rectify. All children can learn to read but this becomes much more difficult and time consuming with each advancing year.

The single most devastating effect in a struggling reader is the child's perception of his ability to learn. He can begin to doubt himself and what he can accomplish. He can begin to stop trying new things because of his fear of failure. He begins to believe that if he cannot learn how to read he must be incapable of doing other things.

He also begins to hate reading which of course impacts his learning in so many more areas. The child needs to read to succeed in every single class. Avoidance of reading, or not being able to read, will lower his self- esteem, limit his learning of new words, limit his self- learning, and can even limit his future potential for advancing in life. He needs to be an efficient reader to obtain an advanced degree or learn a skilled trade.

Yes, a small number of people have been successful without learning how to read, but the ratio is extremely low compared to the number of people who were NOT successful because they could not read. The bottom line is that every child needs to learn to read, and read well, by the time they exit second grade. This goal is attainable.

What does a reading difference look like?

A reading difference (remember, not a disability) can have many different faces. It can be severe or mild and everything in between. All levels of this learning difference have one thing in common: lower achievement for the child. Even a mild reading difference, not rectified, will decrease a child's achievement in some area of his life. Maybe he will avoid reading in front of the class, and later in life, public speaking. Maybe he will avoid learning a skill because it involves a lot of reading and later in life avoid a profession because there was too much reading required to obtain that goal.

A child with a reading difference can display any of the following:

- trouble learning the letters and sounds of the alphabet
- have a difficult time finding a rhyme for a word
- have trouble learning and remembering sight words
- know a sight word one day and not know the word 10 minutes later
- have trouble trying to sound out bigger words
- confuse or replace letters within a word (horse for house)
- When he does start to read, he may know a word in one sentence but not know the same word in the next sentence.
- not be able to recall some or most of what he just read
- Different fonts in books may throw him off completely.
- He may pronounce big words incorrectly, mixing up the order of the syllables (mazagine for magazine).
- He may have no observable trouble with reading in Kindergarten and First grade and then fall far behind in Second grade.
- An older child may show a noticeable difference in what he can tell you orally and what he will write on a test.
- He may read painfully slow and avoid it at all cost. He may learn much better when listening or viewing versus reading.
- The one common factor, in all levels of reading differences in children, is that at some point they all begin to avoid reading. This aversion to reading grows and they begin to fall farther and farther behind, which is the Matthew Effect.

That being said, another factor they all have in common is that they can all improve their reading skills. This learning difference is conquerable.

The Process of Learning to Read

Learning to read is a very complicated and detailed process. When you take a look at everything involved in this process it's a wonder any of us learned how to read. We do learn to read though, because our brain is such a magnificent organ. We are able to take these abstract symbols that we call letters, give them a sound (or 2 or 3 sounds), and combine the sounds to form words. We can then assemble the words into strings of words or sentences to form a coherent thought. When we all learn the same code to decipher the words we can share our knowledge with others and others can learn from us.

This system is advantageous to everyone. Just take a look at the improvements and inventions our society has made in the last 50 years. This is possible because of sharing and building upon past discoveries. A person today can read about another persons' thoughts from hundreds of years ago just by learning the code they used.

All of our brains are "wired" to be able to understand that an abstract symbol can represent something else. Every 5 year old who has seen a tree, can look at a symbol for a tree and know what it is. That is the easy part. Now we take the symbol, [a] for instance and we give it a name, "Aey". Then we give it a sound, /a/ like in "cat" and another sound /ae/ like in "cake" and another sound /aw/ like in tall and sometimes it's even silent like in "coat". (NOTE: This bracket /-/ indicates that the sound of the letter or letters is being discussed.) Now, that alone could make a child want to quit, but then we go on to name 25 more letters. Each letter having its own sound, or sets of sounds. Then we start to combine all these sounds into pairs or groups which can then change the sound, /th/, /sh/, /ch/, /thr/, and on and on. And if all this isn't bad enough, we throw in words from different languages which have their own set of rules and different sounds, for example "tortilla".

I really find it amazing that kindergarten children don't give up. But, luckily, children's brains are very flexible. They are used to not having all the answers and it's not as scary to them as it is to an adult. They just dive in and start learning, chunk by chunk, unless of course there is a learning difference of some kind.

Children with learning differences can still learn to read like all other kids. They just require an explicit type of instruction, and a multisensory learning experience. To understand exactly what your child needs to learn from his reading program, you will need a little background information on the reading process. This will also enable you to monitor whether he is assimilating the instruction or not. If he is not, you can make the appropriate changes to his instruction in a timely manner.

Six Main Areas in Reading

Looking at the reading process, there are 6 main areas to discuss. They are: Letter Naming and Sound Knowledge, Phonemic Awareness, Phonics Rules, Sight Words, Fluency, and Comprehension. Let's take a look at each one and see what it entails.

Letter Naming and Sound Knowledge

First, the child needs to know the name and sound of each letter of the alphabet. Some children learn this naturally, seemingly without effort. Other children find this skill to be an overwhelming struggle. They find it very difficult to hear the subtle differences between many of the sounds, for example, /p/ and /b/ ,and /d/ and /t/. Each of these pairs of sounds is made using the same mouth movements, which makes it even more difficult to tell them apart.

I've had students (and family members) who thought every vowel sounded the same. To them, there was only one vowel sound. They could not discriminate between the subtle sound differences in each vowel. The vowel sound changes the whole word. So, if you only make one vowel sound for every word, you are not going to be very successful in sounding out words accurately and your comprehension will be affected.

Multisensory Methods

A child with learning issues will benefit from using multisensory techniques to help him realize the difference in the sounds and to file and retrieve this information in his brain more effectively. Multisensory methods are very important for efficient learning when there is a learning difference. Multisensory methods are methods that use more than one sense at a time. One example of a multisensory method is to use a tray of course colored sand for the child to trace a letter. The child traces with a finger and repeats the sound at the same time. The child is feeling the coarseness of the sand, seeing the color of the sand, at the same time as he is learning to form the letter and say the sound. This type of learning uses more areas of the brain and gives the child more ways to file and retrieve the information. This is very important for children with learning differences.

Another multisensory method is to use large muscle groups. One way to do this is to have the child close his eyes and write the letter in the air while saying the sound of the letter and using his whole arm to write, not just the hand and wrist. There are many excellent books on this topic, some of which I will include in the appendix.

Using more than one sense to learn the sound helps the child to remember. For example, to help the child learn the difference between /b/ and /p/, I would use several multisensory strategies. First, I would have them take the middle three fingers on each hand and place them on both sides of the vocal cord in his neck. Then I would ask him to make the /b/ sound and feel the vibration in his throat. Next, make the /p/ sound. There is no vibration. I would have him look at a card with the letter written in a bold color while he is making the sound and feeling it in his throat. Now he has sensory information coming in for this sound through his hands (sense of touch), through his eyes (sense of sight), and through his ears, (sense of hearing). I would also have him trace the letter on sandpaper and/or sand tray while saying the sound.

When a child has difficulty telling the difference between sounds, I start the reading instruction by choosing 3-5 sounds that are easily distinguished from each other and are formed in different locations in the mouth or made by different lip movements. This gives the child more information to use and is filed in more locations in the brain which help him to remember the sound. For example I might start with the letters: /t/, /m/, /p/, /s/, and /a/. I work on these sounds using several different multisensory strategies until the child is successful in memorizing them. Memorizing all the letters and sounds in the alphabet at once can be too difficult and intimidating for a child with a learning difference. Children can begin learning to read using only 4 or 5 sounds. The next step is to combine phonemic awareness strategies to these sounds.

Phonemic Awareness

Phonemic awareness is a measure of a child's ability to manipulate sounds in words. Subskills of Phonemic Awareness include, blending sounds, segmenting sounds, deleting and adding sounds, and rhyming words. Research has shown that Phonemic Awareness abilities are a great indicator of reading readiness and ability in young children.

Phonemes are the smallest bit of sound in a word. We combine phonemes to make a word. A child needs to be aware that a word consists of individual phonemes. For example, the word "cat" has 3 distinct phonemes /c/ /a/ and /t/. A child needs to be able to blend these 3 sounds to form the word "cat." A child also needs to be able to segment, or pull apart, these sounds from "cat" to /c/ /a/ /t/. In other words, they need to build a word with separate phonemes (sounds) and pull apart the word by identifying separate phonemes. This is very difficult for a child with an auditory processing difficulty or dyslexia.

Another subskill is the ability to rhyme words. In order to rhyme, you have to delete one or more phonemes and then add a new phoneme. For example, "fat" and "cat". You need to be able to delete the /f/ sound in fat and then add the /c/ sound in its place. While this is very natural and easy for some children, others will find it very difficult.

Phonemic Awareness skills are practiced orally, not visually. The child needs to hear and manipulate spoken sounds. Phonemic Awareness skills can be practiced at a very young age and is actually how language is developed in babies and young children. They are hearing and copying sounds such as /mah/ /mah/, /pah/ /pah/. A child perfects one sound and moves on to the next.

There are approximately 46 phonemes in the English language. Kindergarten children usually know all the sounds in their native language. The skill of reading requires the child to take that sound he already knows, and attach letter symbols. When teaching reading, we start with what the child already knows, the sounds, and begin bit by bit attaching a letter to that sound.

So, can the child make rhyming words such as fat and cat? Can the child blend the sounds /c/ /a/ /t/ into "cat", and segment sounds "cat" into /c/ /a/ /t/? These are the easiest phonemic awareness skills. Deleting and adding sounds in the beginning, middle and end of a word are more advanced phonemic awareness skills and come next. Can the child delete the /m/ from man and tell you what is left (an)? Can the child replace the /m/ in "man" with /f/ and tell you the word (fan)? Can he replace the /a/ sound in "fan" with the /i/ sound (fin)? These phonemic awareness skills will help a child to read and write words.

Once the child knows some sounds and how to segment and blend sounds, he can begin to combine sounds to make words. Two letter combinations can be taught first and are easier to blend and segment, such as "at". Once the child can blend /a/ and /t/ to make "at" we can make a whole list of words using the base "at." These can include: cat, fat, mat, rat, bat, hat, pat, sat, tat, and jat. (You might be asking yourself right now if jat and tat are actually words. They are pretend words. Pretend words are great to use for practicing sounding out words. Then you are sure that the child is really sounding out and not just reading a memorized word. You may have noticed the pretend words in many of the Dr. Seuss books. "At" can be called a word family and words in this family can be made by adding a beginning sound. We can begin using sounds the child is good at and add more sounds one at a time. Now we have a whole word family for the child to practice reading.

When a child is struggling with the sounds of the alphabet, I only use four consonants and one vowel to start. Almost all children can learn four consonant sounds and one vowel sound and then they have several words at their disposal for practicing blending, segmenting and reading skills. When these five sounds are mastered, I add one to two more consonant sounds and make some more word families to practice. Some examples of these word families are: at, an, ap, al, ad, ag, am. A non-reading child becomes highly motivated when they discover they can read a few words. A child can read many, many words using just the few word families above. These words can be put onto cards and read and put into little home-made books and reread. The child begins to develop a more positive attitude to reading when he begins to see some success. The key to being successful here with children who are struggling is to use many multisensory methods and a lot of repetition.

I also emphasize at this time how important the vowel sound is because it changes the whole word. A lot of mistakes are made in the area of the vowel sound, especially with children for whom English is a second language. Eventually, all the vowels and consonants are added and then we start to build bigger word. We also begin to use the "rules" of reading or phonics.

Phonics

Phonics rules are the rules children learn during the first several years of reading instruction. A couple of well know examples of phonics rules are: when 2 vowels go a-walking, the first one does the talking (coat); and silent 'e' at the end of the word will make the vowel sound long or say its name (kite). There was a lot of controversy over the years about using phonics or "whole" language. Both areas have something to offer in the reading process. For right now though, we will just concentrate on the phonics portion.

Phonics teaches the rules to use when decoding more advanced words. These rules at least give the child some tools to use when trying to figure out an unknown word. There are many exceptions to these rules, so some people advocate against learning these rules. I believe the rules at least give a child somewhere to start in attacking the sounding out of the word. The rule usually gets the child close to the actual sounds in the word and when that's combined with using context clues or the meaning of the other words in the sentence, the word can usually be decoded. Phonics rules are usually part of the reading program. They are not learned all at once, but are introduced incrementally as reading skills advance.

There are words which do not follow the phonics rules. Some of these words originated in a different language and follow a different set of rules (i.e.: tortilla). Others are in a group that we call "sight words."

Sight Words

Sight words are words which are seen over and over in all types of reading material and frequently do not follow any phonics rules. Many of the words cannot be sounded out and must be memorized. Knowing the sight words will increase a child's speed in reading and will also help with comprehension. There are many different lists of sight words but the two most common are the Dolch sight word list and the Fry sight word list. Both lists can be found in the appendix and through an internet search. The Fry list consists of 1000 words that can be found in 90% of all print. They are listed in order of frequency in print. The Dolch list consists of 220 words which are all embedded in the Fry list but in a different order. Both lists are useful and both are used in schools. I prefer the Fry list for working with my students.

Flash cards can be made by starting with the first 10 words on the list and adding more as the first ones are memorized. Knowing many sight words and being able to read them quickly helps to improve the child's fluency and comprehension

Fluency

Fluency is how quickly and smoothly a child can read the material. As the material gets more difficult for a child's reading level or ability, the fluency level will decrease. A child will have a low fluency rate when first starting to read, but as he becomes more proficient with the material, his fluency rate will increase.

We can calculate the fluency rate by timing how many words are read in a particular amount of time and how many errors are made. There are charts available in the appendix which will show how to calculate the fluency rate. When a fluency rate is low (slow reading with many errors), comprehension can be adversely affected. If it takes too long to sound out each phoneme in each word, the brain can become overtaxed or distracted, and some of the meaning or comprehension of the material can be lost.

Comprehension

Comprehension means how much of the information being read is understood and remembered. Comprehension can be adversely affected by several factors including: background knowledge of information being read, fluency rate, vocabulary knowledge of information, and interest level of material. For example, a person who has never played golf, and never wants to, might have a lower comprehension level when reading an article based on golf. The person wouldn't have the background knowledge because he never played golf or cared enough to learn about golf. He might not know what some words mean such as "birdie" or "hole in one" because he was never exposed to that information. He might have no interest in golf and find the article boring. All this might contribute to a low fluency rate and low comprehension rate. **The whole purpose of reading anything is to learn something.** Comprehension is the ultimate goal of the reading process.

Points to Ponder

- When learning to read, each "chunk" of information forms the foundation for the next chunk. When there are gaps in the foundation, or incorrect information, the reading process collapses.
- Memorizing words alone, without developing phonics skills, will eventually stall a child's progress in reading.
- A reading difference can present itself with a multitude of different qualities. Every child is unique.
- Every child needs to be a proficient reader by the time they exit second grade. Remember the Matthew Effect.
- The greater the discrepancy between where a child's skills are, and where they should be, the greater the length of time needed to rectify the issue.
- There are 6 main components in learning to read: letter naming and sound knowledge; phonemic awareness; phonics rules; sight words; fluency; comprehension.
- Learning to read is conquerable for everyone!

Chapter 3

Collect Data

"The greatest achievement was, at first, and for a time, but a dream."

James Allen

Now that you have a little background on what is actually involved in learning to read and how to motivate and build up your child's self-esteem, we need to begin addressing your child's unique personal concerns. A few questions we need answered are:

- What does your child know?
- What is your child missing?
- What are your child's strengths and interests?
- What are your child's weaknesses and dislikes?
- What is interfering with your child's ability to acquire reading skills? Is it something physical or some type of learning "disability"?
- Are there self-esteem issues to address? (There usually are, especially in older children.)
- Are there behavior issues to address?
- Are the behavior issues caused by the reading difference or something else?
- Are there food allergies which are interfering with attention span and learning ability?

These questions will be answered during your Data Collection phase. Let's take each question individually, and discuss how to obtain answers.

What Does Your Child Know

First, what does your child know? We want to find out exactly what your child knows so we can use this during the instruction phase. Does your child know any sight words? Does he know any letter names? Does he know any letter sounds? Can he make rhymes or segment sounds or blend sounds? For example, say your child knows the sounds for /b/, /f/, /m/, and /a/ and the sight words "to" and "the". We can start our instruction using this information. We can build a collection of pretend words from these sounds: bam, fam, baf, maf, fab, and mab. These can be written on index cards, along with the 2 sight words. We can practice blending and segmenting each. We can also use letter tiles and have him build and read each word. When all of this becomes easy we can start to add new sounds and sight words. Eventually, we make little books using everything he knows at each point in time and then move on to commercially printed books with controlled sounds and vocabulary. This is just one possible learning plan. Every plan is unique to the child and the child's needs and abilities.

We will begin getting this information from your child's school. Teachers who work with your child can supply the information they have as well as information gathered from any screenings or testing already completed by any school personnel. You will also contribute any information that you know at each stage.

What is Your Child Missing?

Next, what is your child missing? What letters does he not know? What sounds? Which phonemic awareness skills are difficult? Is fluency or comprehension a problem? Are sight words difficult? Is he lacking in phonics skills for his grade level? Is it difficult for him to sit still or to concentrate for long periods? All this information is necessary to put together the best plan for his success. We want to be able to develop a plan that is perfectly suited to your child's unique needs. This information is also gathered by school personnel and includes your contributions.

What Are Your Child's Strengths and Interests?

Next, what are your child's strengths and interests? This information is crucial to building your child's plan for instruction. For example, maybe your child loves everything to do with horses such as care, feeding, exercising, breeds, etc. This information can be used in two ways.

First, the instructor could gather any literature available on horses for reading together and developing lesson plans. The letters h,o,r,s, and e could be learned first and words made from these letters combined with any letters your child already knows. You will be able to keep him focused longer on reading if you use material that is personally interesting to him.

The second way to use this information is as a motivator. Maybe you can offer to get horseback riding lessons as an incentive. For every 10 lessons, he earns one horseback riding lesson, or whatever you decide. Use this to suit both of your needs (and your bank account of course). You could offer to take him to a petting zoo to feed ponies. Anything that will motivate him during this time can increase his rate of progress. You can fit this learning plan to your child's unique personality by incorporating any subject or talent that is of interest to him. You can be very inventive in personalizing the instruction by using materials and methods that uniquely work for your child.

What Are Your Child's Weaknesses and Dislikes?

Now, what are your child's weaknesses and dislikes? We want to make sure that the instruction is not squarely placed on any weakness or dislikes. The weakness can be built up gradually but should not be used in the beginning when setting up a new instruction plan. For example, your child hates writing anything on paper with a pencil. Then use dry erase boards, or chalk boards or a tray filled with colored sand. Have him air write using his whole arm. Then it is more like drawing rather than writing. Or your child hates the color pink. Then have all your materials in different colors. I know this sounds so immaterial when you are looking at the big picture of your child not reading, but incorporating these little things into your instruction makes it easier for your child to concentrate and helps to avoid any unnecessary distractions that always lead to trouble. You want to use as much personal information as possible to make this instruction perfectly suited to this child. This information will come from the school personnel as well as the parent.

What is interfering with Your Child's Learning?

Now, what is interfering with your child's ability to acquire reading skills? Does this involve a health issue, physical issue, or hereditary component? Does it involve a psychological component? Have you moved or divorced recently? Does it involve a cognitive component or learning difference? Each different scenario needs to be ruled out or confirmed during this phase of the investigation. Does a close relative have a reading difficulty? Dyslexia is hereditary. Maybe your child has a speech, hearing, or vision issue that hasn't been detected yet. Any of these issues would affect learning and should (but not always) be discovered at this time.

People kept telling me that my daughter had a hearing problem because of different behaviors she was exhibiting. I had her hearing tested three times and it was always perfect. It turned out she had a Central Auditory Processing issue that needed to be addressed. This issue manifests in many different ways. My daughter's symptoms included; mispronouncing multisyllabic words (bizgetti for spaghetti, mazageen for magazine), only able to remember and complete one task from a list of three or four, always needing the person to look at her when they were talking so she could understand them, could not spell correctly, could not read, could not remember sight words, and more. The audiologist who evaluated her uncovered the fact that she was lip reading to help her compensate for a difficulty in auditory functioning in her brain.

This part of the assessment will be completed by a team of professionals at the school, and may include, but is not limited to, any of the following: school nurse, psychologist, reading specialist, speech therapist, physical therapist, occupational therapist, teachers assigned to your child, and the building principal. These assessments may also point to the need for further review and assessment by a professional outside of school.

Self-Esteem Issues

Frequently there are self-esteem issues attached to a reading difficulty. The child sees other kids learning easily and he cannot do it at all. Other students might be making fun of him. This is also common. Kids can be mean and it tends to be worse in the upper grades. You can rectify this with a lot of encouragement at home by the parents and at school by the teachers. When the child starts to see success, his self-esteem begins to increase.

My daughter had great self-esteem at home but when I went to observe her in a school setting in second grade, she was sitting slumped down in her chair with her hair blocking her face. I was shocked. At home she was very confident. Once we addressed the learning difference, she was confident in school and her self-esteem skyrocketed.

Behavior Issues

The behavior issue topic is difficult for parents. No one wants to think their child has a behavior problem. This can be caused by a number of issues including: low self-esteem, allergies and food intolerances, bad habits, not enough sleep, or poor nutrition. Whatever the cause, the fact that it exists should come up during the assessment phase by school personnel as well as parents.

A plan must be put in place to address this issue. There is always a cause for behavior issues. Once the cause is uncovered, it can be addressed. For example, a child can have rages when he has a gluten intolerance or dairy intolerance. When you eliminate the offending food or foods from the diet, the rages subside. People do not seem to be aware of how detrimental a food intolerance or food allergy can be to a child's disposition, behavior and learning ability. You need to do some detective work to uncover this type of problem.

Please do not be too quick to put your child on medication. This is a very touchy subject for many people but one that needs to be discussed. Someone can very easily say that your child cannot focus and has ADD or ADHD and needs medicine. Frequently we are offered medicine that will address symptoms but not address the underlying condition. While it is much easier to take a pill and mask a symptom, it's much healthier (mentally and physically) in the long run to get to the root of the problem and resolve it. Also, all medicine has side effects. Sometimes the side effects are much worse than the actual condition. There is a place for medicine, of course, but it should be as a last resort not the first one. I know of hundreds of cases where prescription medicine was avoided by implementing a change in diet and/or a adding a quality nutritional supplement.

I was told many times that my daughter needed to be on medicine for ADD. I did not believe she had ADD and looked into other possibilities. Her symptoms all went away when she went gluten free and added a nutritional supplement to her diet. She had Celiac Disease, not ADD. So, because I was investigating why my daughter could not learn how to read, I uncovered that she had CAPD (Central Auditory Processing Disorder), Celiac Disease, and dyslexia. No wonder she struggled in school. If I had put her on medicine, all her symptoms would have been masked as well as altered which would have made finding out the truth even more difficult.

When you are looking into behavior problems, look into all possible causes before accepting medicine. During this phase of the investigation you will have input from school personnel assessments as well as medical assessments if necessary. You are still the parent and will make the final decision about medicine. Please do your research here. Try as many things as you can before you resort to medicine.

Optimal Nutrition Using a Nutritional Supplement

If you are worried about your child's health like I used to be, contact me at: www.TheReadingTutor.org and I will share a product I market that worked for my family. My younger daughter had bronchitis and pneumonia repeatedly from the age of two to four. She also caught every cold and flu that came along which meant that the rest of my family caught every cold and flu. I tried vitamin pills, juicing, tons of fruits and vegetables, but nothing seemed to work. She was missing so much school, which meant that I was missing so much work, that I thought I would lose my job. We seemed to be stuck in the house all winter long trying to recover from the latest illness. The scary part of all this was the amount of antibiotics my family was consuming in a year. I was extremely concerned about our future health, especially if we had to rely on so many antibiotics to keep us out of the hospital. I was desperate to break this cycle.

About ten years ago my sister told me about a nutritional product to try, which I did. I was surprised when my daughter did not get sick that month. Over the course of that winter she caught a couple of colds and coughs but nothing developed into anything serious like it usually did. This was her first winter without any antibiotics, as well as the first winter the rest of my family did not take an antibiotic. It has now been over seven years since this little girl has been on any medicine. I talked to hundreds of parents along my journey with this business whose children have had life changing results with these products. I feel compelled to offer you the same opportunity. This might just be another piece to your puzzle and is worth investigating.

Food Allergies

Food allergies and food intolerance can interfere with attention span, moodiness, anger outbursts, sleep patterns, and learning abilities, as well as a host of other issues. Have your child screened for these. Your insurance should cover the fee for this test and it is time well spent. People are not always aware of the extent of the behavior and health issues that can be cleared up by a change in diet. It can be miraculous. This is just one more piece to examine. This phase is usually completed by a physician with parental input. And, please remember, you do not have to do prescription medicine. Check out all the possibilities first.

Learning Disability Diagnosis

Don't worry about a learning disability diagnosis. It sounds so scary thinking your child may have a learning disability. Remember to focus on this being a learning "difference" not a "disability". But don't think of this as a deficit in your child. There are always many assets included in this diagnosis. A child with a learning difference often has great strengths in another area. You will discover these strengths along the way. Remember, your first job as a parent is to encourage, encourage, and encourage some more. The gifts will show themselves when your child is confident.

Professional Screenings Outside School Setting

Have your child evaluated by a physician for any allergies or food intolerances, as well as for any underlying physical conditions which could impact learning. You also might need to do additional testing, depending on the results you receive.

My daughter's school district was not equipped to diagnose or work with an auditory processing disability. I did research on my own and came to the conclusion that she needed to see an audiologist. That is when I learned that she had Central Auditory Processing Disorder (CAPD).

Every district varies in availability of screening options. You will possibly need to see a professional outside the school district depending on your child's unique situation.

Research Your Diagnosis

Lastly, research any diagnosis you are given. Professionals are not infallible. Mistakes do happen and you do not want a mistaken diagnosis with your child. Make sure you definitely agree with the diagnosis you are given. Do not just blindly accept anyone's diagnosis unless you feel it truly fits your child's situation. The worst scenario at this time is for you to follow a plan based on an erroneous diagnosis. You know your child best. You should know if this diagnosis fits your child's symptoms. You can find a wealth of information on the internet to check and compare all the information which you are given.

You need to satisfactorily answer all the pertinent questions concerning the following: your child's health; background; strengths; weaknesses; learning style; learning differences; and interests or hobbies. Then you will move on to the next phase, which is planning your method of instruction.

Points to Ponder

- Obtain answers to all of the following that pertain to your child's unique situation: What does your child know?; What is your child missing?; What are your child's strengths and interests?; What are your child's weaknesses and dislikes?; What is interfering with your child's ability to acquire reading skills?; Is there something physical causing an issue or some type of learning difference?; Are there self-esteem issues to address?; Are there behavior issues to address?; Are the behavior issues caused by the reading difference or something else?; Are there food allergies which are interfering with attention span and/or learning ability?

- Data collection must be thorough and accurate to effectively guide the learning process.

- Consult professionals on issues pertaining to your child but also personally investigate all diagnoses.

- Make sure you completely agree with all diagnoses as fitting your child's unique situation. Your child's success or lack of success will depend on this.

- Food allergies and intolerances **can** and **do** affect learning. Investigate this aspect also.

- A quality nutritional product can result in a life changing difference. Contact me for more information on what worked for my family at: www.TheReadingTutor.org .

Chapter 4

The IEP Meeting (Individualized Education Program)

*"I can be what I **will** to be"*

Charles Haanel

Public Law 94-142

A law was enacted in 1975 called "Education for all Handicapped Children Act" or Public Law 94-142. You can perform an internet search to learn about your rights as a parent, which are protected by this law. This law guarantees a "free, appropriate public education to each child with a disability in every state and localities across the country." The education must be provided in an environment that is considered to be the least restrictive for the child. This law covers children with all degree of handicaps and disabilities. A child who is having trouble learning to read could possibly have a learning difference (stated as disability in this piece of legislature) which is causing an interference with his learning to read. This learning difference can be covered under this law.

A parent or teacher can recommend that a child be evaluated when they believe that something is interfering with the child's educational progress. According to Public Law 94-142, the child needs to be evaluated by a professional team at the school. The personnel involved in the testing will depend on the child's specific needs. If the evaluation results show that there is some type of learning difference, which is having a direct impact on the child's learning progress, the multidisciplinary team is required to write an IEP for the child.

An IEP is an Individualized Education Program. The IEP plan is required to identify the type of disability that is impacting the child's learning, as well as give educational guidelines to follow which would help the child reach his highest level of success. The plan is required to be in the least restrictive environment according to the child's personal and specific needs. In other words, the education plan needs to blend into the child's typical daily school routine as much as possible.

Different Levels for Least Restrictive Environment

The first example for an accommodation in the least restrictive environment would be an accommodation in the classroom. This can be extra assistance in the classroom given by an aide or specialist. This is the lowest level of restrictive environment. Another example at this level is extra time to take a test. The child's daily classroom routine is not being challenged at this level.

The next level of least restrictive environment is pulling the child out of the classroom for extra help in a resource room, in the same building, during the regular school day. The child's daily classroom routine is being altered but only slightly. The child is with fellow classmates for the majority of the day.

The next level would be pulling the child out of the regular classroom for an extended portion of the day. The child in this situation studies some of his subjects with the homeroom class and other subjects with a specialist or another class. This type of accommodation is suited for children whose learning difference affects their learning in a specific area and would benefit from more intense instruction outside the typical classroom. A child on the autism spectrum might benefit from this type of accommodation.

The most restrictive environment could include a self-contained classroom including only children with similar needs or challenges. This is considered extremely restrictive because the children do not interact with other children who do not have challenges of some sort. This does not happen too often in today's school system. Most children can be involved in a regular classroom for some portion of the day. The most restrictive environment would usually only occur for the child's safety, or fellow students' safety.

Public Law 94-142 has been successful in improving the quality of education for children with learning differences and challenges.

Assessment Request

Let us take a look at how this impacts a child who is having trouble learning to read. Usually, the parent or teacher will notice that the child is struggling. The teacher can be the first one to request that the child be tested, but the school must receive the parents' permission in writing before any testing can be pursued. The parent can also request testing. The first person to go to would be the child's teacher. The teacher can then begin the process of formally requesting an evaluation of the child's ability to learn. Children attending private schools, or children who are home-schooled by their parents, are evaluated by the public school in the district where they reside and pay taxes. The child's teacher should know who to contact in this situation but if not, the parent can contact their local public school and ask for this information.

Once in agreement that the child requires an evaluation, the process begins. The teacher contacts the person in charge of the evaluation and that person contacts the parent. This contact usually occurs with a phone call and then paperwork follows for the parent to sign giving permission for the school to complete the evaluation.

The parent's paperwork will include their observations of the child's learning styles and difficulties. The parent will also include a health history and any information pertinent to the evaluation. These forms are sent back to the person in charge of the testing or team leader.

Next to be determined involves what type of evaluation is needed for this child. Any specialist deemed necessary for this situation is then notified. This reading situation might involve a reading specialist, school psychologist, nurse for health, vision and hearing screening, a social worker, teacher and parent. Each situation and district will vary as to who is involved. The specialists then contact the parent to set up a time and place for their end of the evaluation. The evaluation can occur during school time as well as after school.

Once each specialist completes their portion of the testing, the team leader will compile all the information into one report and call the parent to set up the meeting. This is the IEP meeting. The team decides if the child requires an IEP plan based on the findings from the evaluations of all the team members. The parent receives a written copy of the testing results and observations made by each team member.

IEP Meeting

Next, the IEP meeting occurs. Every team member involved in the evaluation process is invited to attend and present their findings. The parent is also a big part of this meeting. Please do not be intimidated by a room full of specialists. You are the child's parent and hold the most pertinent information of all the team members. You belong in that meeting and you are a major component of that meeting.

Everyone on the team sits around a table. Each specialist will have a copy of their testing results in front of them. One by one, each will be given time to present what they found. A pen and paper will be very helpful for you to write down any questions or concerns you think of while you are listening to their findings. Do not expect to remember everything that is said. You will be hearing a lot of information and some of it might not be clear to you. Especially if you hear something you did not expect. Some of the language being used might be new to you. Just write down any questions or concerns as you think of them and you can discuss them at some point after hearing what was learned.

After everyone presents their findings, they discuss whether an instructional plan is warranted. The plan is set up at this time if it is found to be necessary. You can also have input into this plan. Think about what you want for your child. Think about how your child learns best, as well as his interests and dislikes. The child's plan can take all this into account and be adjusted according to your suggestions. You must have an idea of all this before you sit down at this table. Do your research beforehand.

If you hear findings you did not expect, you can research them yourself after this meeting and decide on the best course of action for your child at a later date. This plan is not set in stone. It can be adjusted and amended along the way.

The parent has certain rights which are protected by Public Law 94-142. The parent has the right to be involved in this whole process and to voice their concerns or objections about any course of action discussed in this meeting. The parent's input is very important to the success of this meeting because he knows his child better than any other person in that meeting. The meeting is to present findings and decide on the best course of action for your child.

You have the right to contribute to your child's education plan. Know what you want for your child before the meeting. Go into the meeting with an open mind. Listen to all the findings carefully. Think about what is best for your child. You can challenge any decisions concerning your child's education. This is your right as the parent. The whole reason for this meeting is to decide on a plan of action that is best suited to your child's individual needs. The result of this plan is supposed to be your child's highest level of success in the academic program. Voice your disagreement during this meeting so adjustments can be considered or the reasons given why they cannot be considered. This is the time for complete understanding between the parent and the team to ensure your child's highest level of success.

You can also ask to make changes to your child's program later on if you notice your child is not making progress. Keep in touch with whoever is in charge of implementing your child's IEP plan.

I participated in this process as a parent and as a Reading Specialist. When I attended the meeting as a parent, I was extremely intimidated. When I attended the meeting as a professional, I observed other parents who were extremely intimidated. Often times, the parent did not want to voice any concerns because he did not view himself as an "expert". I felt the same way. Do not feel intimidated. You are an expert concerning your child. Your input is crucial to the success of this meeting as well as the success of your child.

My First IEP Meeting as a Parent

My first experience of an IEP meeting was very intimidating and upsetting. I did not agree with the results presented by the team in place at that school at that particular time. I did not realize at this time that I could question their results or have input into my daughter's IEP plan. Consequently, this plan was not effective and had a negative impact on my daughter's reading progress. She was subjected to many questionable assessments and modifications to her school work during this time. Not one person on that particular team was qualified to diagnose or treat a CAPD (Central Auditory Processing Disorder). I assumed that they were the experts. Do not assume anything at this stage. You can question anything you are uncertain about. Eventually, I realized that this plan was not working for my daughter and I sought further testing outside my school district. I then found a program that would work for her based on the results of testing by an audiologist.

I do not share this information to bash a school district. I share it to help you to avoid some of the mistakes I made which cost my daughter extra crucial time in learning to read. Every situation and district will vary. You have to be involved in every step of the process to ensure that the final result is beneficial to your child. Your child's success is always the most important aspect of any scenario. Don't just blindly accept whatever is offered. Be an active, verbal participant in your child's education.

I just recently participated in my younger daughter's IEP meeting. This was a totally different scenario and very productive. I am not sure if this meeting was different because I have more experience with IEP meetings at this stage in my life, or this district follows different guidelines, or maybe it was due to the team members involved? The reason probably is due to a combination of all of the above. I do know the two meetings were at polar opposites of the spectrum.

An Actual IEP Meeting

I will share exactly what occurred in this recent IEP meeting to give you an idea of what this process and meeting can look like. First, I will give you a little background information. My younger child had a very difficult time learning to read at the kindergarten level. She was also dealing with severe separation anxiety and I was not sure if this was contributing to her issue with reading or not.

Her early years most likely contributed to all the trouble. She was born in China and lived in an orphanage until she was two years old. Her caretaker would leave every day at 5 which was very traumatic for my daughter and probably caused the beginning of the separation anxiety. Then I came to China and picked her up. I brought her to America where none of us even spoke her language. She was immersed into a totally different culture and environment which would be a shock to anyone's system.

From the very beginning, my daughter was anxious whenever anyone left her presence. This person could even be a stranger like a UPS driver or the mailman. She was eventually diagnosed with separation anxiety.

The separation anxiety became very severe during kindergarten. It was so bad that I was advised to keep her home from school and as close to me as possible until she recovered. I resigned from my job and home-schooled her at this time. I taught her to read during kindergarten and first grade using several multisensory reading programs, materials, and methods. I became aware of her learning difficulties during this time and decided to have her tested by an audiologist since she had many similar learning styles as my older daughter.

The audiologist identified a learning issue that involved the global processing in her brain. This issue was not severe enough at this time to require intervention. The audiologist recommended that I continue to observe my daughter's progress and told me who to call if necessary. She also agreed that my daughter's background was a major contributing factor to her learning issues.

My daughter went back into a private school at the second grade level. She was still a little behind the other students, but was progressing wonderfully, so I did not have her tested any further. I also continued to work with her at home.

IEP Process Begins

During a parent teacher conference, my child's third grade teacher recommended having her tested for learning disabilities. She believed my daughter's inconsistencies in the classroom warranted further testing. Her grades at this time were A's, B's, and C's.

I personally do not think a child needs straight A's to be successful. I was happy with her progress but I agreed to the testing because I knew it would not harm her self-esteem and could actually shed more light on identifying her strengths and weakness. This, in turn, would help us to help her reach her full potential. This conversation started the whole IEP process.

The Learning Resource teacher at my daughter's school sent home forms for me to sign. These forms gave my consent to the testing which I signed and returned. The forms were then sent to the public school connected with our private school district. Since my daughter attends a private school, the law in our district requires that the school nearest her private school perform the assessments and the IEP plan but not to implement the plan. The public school connected to my home address would be required to implement the actions in the plan if any were warranted. These rules vary from district to district but your school personnel will be able to explain your particular situation.

My consent forms were forwarded to the public school in charge of the testing and I received a call from their school psychologist. She mailed me more consent forms and a document with information concerning the school district's intervention guidelines. She also gave me information over the phone on what to expect for testing and an approximate time line for completing all the assessments. She was very helpful and gave me her phone number in case I had any further questions.

The testing then began. Some assessments were completed during school hours at my daughter's school. Other assessments were completed at the public school. We set up times after school hours for these tests. The school social worker completed the Social Development Study over the phone. He asked me questions, which I answered, and then a report was completed and typed up.

The assessments were completed in approximately 6 weeks. I then received a form notifying me of the date for the conference, or IEP meeting. This document gave me the time of the conference and the names of all the personnel that were invited to attend. Included in this packet was a copy the results of all the assessments.

I was able to look this information over before the conference and write down any questions I had. This packet of forms included: a Consent to Assess which included a chart identifying educational concerns and who would be doing each assessment, assessment results compiled by my daughter's private school, my original signed consent form, a "Comprehensive Evaluation Referral/Request form that the Learning Resource teacher sent from my daughter's school, reports from the school nurse including hearing and vision screening, a Social Development Study completed by the school social worker (this was completed via a phone interview and then typed up), Academic History and Current Educational Functioning form completed by the classroom teacher, Speech Language Case History completed by the speech pathologist, a psychological report completed by the school psychologist, and the Parent/Guardian Notification of Conference form.

Finally, I attended the IEP meeting. I brought my packet of papers that I received in the mail, as well as my written questions. Since this meeting convened in the summer months, several members of the team were not able to attend. I was given forms to sign which showed that I agreed to hold this meeting without these members. The members were not pertinent to my daughter's situation so this was not an issue.

All the members sat around a long table. Each member of the team had a copy of the report on assessments. I was given another copy of the paperwork I received in the mail pertaining to all the assessment results. Each member of the team was then given the opportunity to discuss their results and I was able to have all my questions answered.

Results of IEP Meeting

The team concluded that my daughter did indeed have a learning issue which appeared to be negatively impacting her progress in mathematics and test taking. Her learning difference involved visual perception, short term memory and processing speed. As a team, we discussed ways to improve her learning environment that would help her uncover her true abilities. Recommendations were suggested, discussed, and agreed upon. Overall, this was an exceptional learning experience for me. This testing was extremely helpful for helping me to understand my daughter's abilities, strengths, and weaknesses and for making adjustments to her learning environment which would be beneficial to her success. This was the information I needed to continue to help her reach her full potential.

Since the learning specialist at my daughter's school was not able to attend this meeting, we held a meeting when school reconvened. She received a copy of the report and had specific recommendations for strategies to implement in the classroom. A couple of suggestions included: more time for tests in the future if it is needed, a chart with the multiplication table for use during math class and test taking, and desk placement nearer to the teacher. More strategies would be discussed in the future, if necessary.

There were several important results from this assessment process. First, I learned my daughter had a visual perception issue. I had no idea. Now I can research this issue and address it outside of school if needed. Next, the testing confirmed my suspicion about a short term memory issue. This issue did not seem to be severe enough to have a major impact on her learning. Slight modifications in her classroom should address this issue. Most importantly, we made a few adjustments in school that took some of the pressure off her. For example, since short term memory is an issue, she is allowed to use a multiplication table during her math test. This is a great scaffold for her until she memorizes the multiplication facts. This small adjustment also greatly reduces her anxiety during math class. These small adjustments can make a world of difference.

Finally, it was wonderful to be part of this whole process, not just an observer. I had a voice in my daughter's education plan which was very important to me. I did not want to subject her to conditions that I knew she would hate and might have a negative impact on her learning.

Testing can be subjective. Results can sometimes be interpreted differently by different personalities, especially if the assessment results only show a mild or moderate learning difference. The child could be having a bad day. The person doing the testing could be having a bad day. I would hate to subject my daughter to an intervention program based on erroneous testing results. This meeting gave me the chance to discuss options with a group of professionals that all had my daughter's best interest at heart. This is how an IEP meeting is meant to function.

Recap Investigation by IEP Team

Let's recap your investigation. First, you need to find out as much information as possible about your child. You need to inform your school personnel (start with your child's teacher) that you want a complete battery of tests to be performed by the school to check if your child has a learning difference. The tests in the school will be performed by a variety of school personnel. These will also be the people who attend the meeting between you and the school. This meeting is called the IEP meeting. The IEP stands for: Individualized Education Program. This plan can include information from any of the following areas:

- Health history, eye exam and hearing test to be completed by the nurse
- Cognitive Functioning completed by school psychologist or special education team which includes reading, math, writing, and problem solving skill assessments or testing
- Communication status which is evaluated by the Speech Pathologist
- Motor abilities completed by special education team
- Academic achievement data collection collected by the child's teacher which includes past report card grades
- A Social Worker will also usually assess current and past issues that might be contributing factors

The tests results will be presented and explained to the parent during an IEP meeting. This meeting can be intimidating for a parent, but can also give a wealth of information which the parent can then use when deciding on the next step. You will decide on any further testing outside of school after you attend this meeting and evaluate for yourself what was uncovered and discussed during this meeting. Next we will discuss your options for choosing a reading program based on what you now know from the results of the assessments.

Points to Ponder

- According to Public Law 94-142, a child with a documented reading difficulty is entitled to extra help and modifications to the curriculum according to his needs.
- The parents also have constitutional rights during this process which are outlined in the document.
- The IEP meeting process can be initiated by a parent or a teacher with a parents' written consent.
- An IEP plan is a plan which alters or modifies a child's educational curriculum based on the child's needs. These needs are determined during the IEP meeting.
- Every IEP meeting does not conclude with an IEP plan. The plan is determined by need.

Chapter 5

Evaluate Options

"Obstacles are those frightening things you see when you take your eyes off the target"

Henry James

You finally have:

- acquired all your child's assessment results
- attended your child's IEP meeting
- listened to recommendations given by all the professionals
- completed your own research on the computer
- checked out all your questions with professionals outside of school, including: audiologist, school psychologist, reading specialist, speech therapist, physician, educational consultant, and any professional who specifically applies to your child's situation.

Remember, you can always get a second opinion from a trained professional outside your school setting. You do not have to take the first opinion as being the gold standard for truth concerning your child's potential. And, as always, your opinion as a parent counts. You know your child best.

Now you have a decision to make. Who is going to be responsible for implementing a reading program for your child? You have 3 choices here. They are:

1) Leave this up to the school. Accept what they offer for your child's reading development.
2) Pay for a private party to address your child's reading development, after school hours.
3) Implement a reading program on your own, at home.

We will discuss the pros and cons of each one separately.

```
┌─────────────────────────────────────────────────────────────────┐
│                   Choice 1 – Accept School Program                │
│                                                                   │
│  Pros:   Less time involved                                       │
│                                                                   │
│          No extra out of pocket expense                           │
│                                                                   │
│          Easiest choice                                           │
│                                                                   │
│  Cons:   May not be successfully matched to your child's needs    │
│                                                                   │
│          Must accept what is available, not much choice offered   │
│                                                                   │
│          May take time away from other subjects in school         │
└─────────────────────────────────────────────────────────────────┘
```

Pros of School Program

The two most obvious pros are less time involvement of parent and no extra cost to parent. This is the easiest choice. You do not have to put out any extra money or take time out of a hectic schedule to make room for a reading appointment outside of school time. Your involvement mainly requires you to follow your child's reading progress by attending any conferences and reading with your child at night before bed. Working parents are very hard pressed for time. Adding one more activity to an already full schedule might just be too much to take on at this time, which makes this choice look very appealing.

School districts are extremely diverse with regards to their reading programs and what "extras" they have to offer to a struggling reader. You will have to personally check out what your school has to offer. If you belong to a well-funded district, then chances are your school has a great intervention program in place.

Three Tier Intervention Program in School

A good intervention program will have leveled tiers of intervention. In other words, the program will have several different platforms of intervention, depending on the specific reading level of the student. Each tier, or level, allots a different amount of time to the intervention as well as different sizes of the groups, and a different form of intervention plan. There are usually 3 tiers or levels in this program.

The third tier is a more intense intervention with more time devoted to the interventions, lower teacher to student ratios, and frequent assessment. One on one intervention is best at this stage and you may see 30-60 minutes of intervention a day, five days a week (in addition to the regular classroom reading instruction time.)

The next level, the second tier, will have less time given to interventions and possibly more children in the group. The largest group should have no more than a 6 to 1 child to teacher ratio, and the time allotted may be 30-60 minutes a day, three days a week instead of five.

The first tier has the least amount of time given to the interventions and has a higher child to teacher ratio, still with 6 to 1 student to teacher ratio being the highest. This level might be once or twice a week for 30 minutes. This is just one example of a 3 tier program. Each program will vary somewhat from school to school. The whole premise of the program is to allow more intense and aligned instruction for the children who need this the most. This instruction adjusts in time, frequency, and material, as the child increases his skills. This instruction continues until the child reaches a predetermined level. This is a much better approach than the "one size fits all" approach. Students' needs are different so the support offered needs to be different.

What to Look For in a Quality School Intervention Program

The amount of intervention per day/week should vary according to the unique needs of the individual learner and the plan in place at the school. There are many different intervention programs but the good ones all have several things in common:

- low student to teacher ratios;
- more individual instruction according to child's unique needs, not vague general needs;
- one-on-one instruction or small groups of children with similar instructional needs;
- a different way of presenting instruction that differs from the original instruction;
- daily or weekly assessments to check if intervention is working;
- a flexible plan that can make room for child's unique needs and make adjustments accordingly;
- daily extended time devoted to intervention, in addition to regular classroom reading time;
- preferably using multisensory instruction;
- instruction that is systematic and progressive;
- instruction that has clear goals and objectives;
- And last but not least, is led by a teacher who specializes in reading.

You do not want an intervention that only includes placing your child on a computer doing a reading program. You want to see one-on-one intervention with a qualified reading instructor for any intense interventions. This will not be a one size fits all approach. It will be individualized and based on the personal needs of your child.

What to Look For at Home For the Duration of the School Intervention

Accept the school option if it supports a quality intervention program. But, do not just sit back and think you have taken care of your child's reading issues. Now you have to closely monitor your child's progress. Are you seeing success at home? Is your child's attitude to reading changing? Is he more receptive to reading with you at night? Be ready to make changes if this is not working. Do not wait a year or more to see improvement. You should see some improvement within a couple of weeks.

Cons of School Program

The first con for this approach is that it may not be successful. A poorly funded district will not have the money or manpower to implement a strong intervention program. Many "extras" are cut when funding is low and this is very likely in times with a struggling economy. There are always exceptions though. Principals are always trying to find ways to increase their funding and improve their schools. You will have to check with your school and make sure that the program you need is being offered, and that it is being implemented by a person explicitly trained in this area.

You will also have to make sure that what is being offered is not just a repeat of what your child was not successful with in the first place. Sometimes the intervention program can look good on paper but the delivery of the program is not actually what it is supposed to be. This can occur because of time constraints, money constraints, scheduling difficulties, a teacher's unplanned extended absence or any of a variety of reasons. You will have to be diligent in checking that your child is getting what has been approved and in the full quantity and quality discussed and approved by all parties.

There is so much variety in what is being offered from school to school and district to district. The only way to ensure that the program will benefit your child is to do your research and be aware of your child's progress. You do not want to become complacent and allow too much time to go by with no progress. (Remember the Matthew Effect). Time is of the essence here.

Another con is that the program being offered might include pulling your child out of other classes to fit the extra reading time into the schedule. Are you OK with this? What other class or classes is your child missing and can he afford to miss instruction time in this class? These are very important considerations. For example, can your child afford to miss several mathematics classes a week if this is the only time available to offer an extra reading program? If not, then you might have to look at a program during after school hours. The school personnel do not want this to happen any more than you but sometimes the logistics of taking into account several people's daily and weekly schedules affords no choice.

Choice 2 – Pay Private Party

PROS: **More freedom in choosing specific program**

Can match program to child's specific needs

Can raise child's reading levels quicker and be more effective than a school program

CONS: **Can be extremely costly**

Can be time consuming

Requires more personal commitment

Requires research into programs' credentials and how they match with child's needs

Pros of Private Party

This option gives you more freedom to choose what your child will be doing and who will be working with him. This option can be more closely matched to your child's specific needs, especially important when your child's school program does not. There are two ways to receive instruction when you are paying a private party:

- A tutor trained in a specific program who comes to your home;
- A clinic where you bring your child and which offers specifically trained personnel to implement the instruction according to specific guidelines.

Both choices can be effective as long as the specific program fits your child's specific needs, the personnel are highly trained and have a personality that works well with your child's personality. Your home needs to be conducive to learning and not too distracting for the child, if you choose the home option. So, if you have several dogs, 8 kids, and one child who plays the drums, the home option might not be the best for you.

Rule of Thumb for Choosing a Program

This may all sound confusing so let me give you a good rule of thumb. If your child is more than 1 grade level behind and/or has a severe learning issue in reading, use a professional program with highly trained personnel. If your child is less than 1 year behind in reading, does not seem to be struggling too much in other subjects, and does not have a severe learning issue, a reading tutor or parent can implement the program. As with any program, be on the look-out for progress. If you do not see sufficient progress, take action. Make changes to the program or to who is delivering the program.

What to Look For in a Quality Program

A qualified instructor in any program will take your child's personal needs, history, and learning difference into account when planning and implementing his instruction. A qualified instructor should also be able to test your child to discern his reading level, sight word level, comprehension level, phonemic awareness level, fluency level, and possibly vocabulary level.

The instructor should be able to sit down with you and explain the testing results and the plan of action he will be following. He should also be able to explain how he is going to assess your child's progress and how often during the implementation of the program. Regular conversations should be occurring between you and the instructor. And as always, are you seeing progress at home? If not, find out why. Changes need to be made if you are not seeing progress.

The setting for this type of instruction can occur in your home, the tutor's home, library, storefront, or clinic. A tutor coming to your home is usually the easiest option but is also the most expensive if the tutor is highly trained.

Lindamood-Bell and Wilson are two good choices when your child is more than 1 year behind in reading or has a severe learning issue. Both of these programs involve explicit training for their instructors in very specific formats and are extremely effective with a child having a severe learning issue. Both of these programs offer in home services but at a higher cost. You can always inquire if you would rather the convenience of someone coming to you verses you having to go to them.

Both programs can increase your child's reading scores faster and more effectively than in a school setting for many reasons. First, there is frequently more instructor accountability. This person is being paid solely on the work he is accomplishing with your child. If he is not an effective instructor, he is fired. There is also a much smaller case load for the private instructor versus the instructor in the school system. This makes it easier to catch and rectify a problem.

Secondly, the instructor has been specifically trained and tested in this particular reading program. He knows what to do and what modifications to make in order to be successful. A certified teacher may or may not be trained in a specific reading program. This training is not usually required.

Finally, the program can be more closely matched to your child's specific needs. You can choose the correct program whereas in the school you have to accept what's offered. If the program in your child's school matches your child's needs, then great, you're in luck. If not, research what is available in your area that better suits your child.

Cons to Private Program

There are mainly two cons to this approach;

- cost
- time commitment.

The first is the cost. You usually pay by the hour, although some do offer weekly or monthly plans which qualify for additional savings. The hourly cost is anywhere from $40-$80 US dollars, more when they come to your home.

The second con is the time constraint on you. You will have to drive your child to his session, wait for the session to be completed and then drive home. You will have to do this 1-5 days a week and anywhere from a couple of months to a year or more. The length of time all depends on your child's age, how far behind he is, and the severity of the learning issue. This can all be very overwhelming to a parent. But please, just remember it's temporary and very necessary for your child's ultimate success.

Choosing a Program on Your Own

If you find a program not mentioned above that you want to use, do some research into the programs' credentials and how they fit with your child's personal needs. The program you choose must be research based and proven to be effective. There are many programs that make claims but do not have quality research supporting them.

There are tutoring outfits in storefronts that make claims to raise grade levels, guaranteed. Many of these are just a repeat of instruction that your child was given in school. If you are using one of these, you have to take a good look at their methods of instruction and the actual program they are using. These outfits may be good for one type of learner but not another. If your child is behind because he missed a lot of school, or is a slow learner and needs to see material again, or maybe just missed a couple of necessary skills, then this might be an option for you. But if your child has a specific learning difference such as CAPD, dyslexia, or autism, you need to make sure the material being used and the method of instruction suits your child's needs.

Example of Instruction not Meeting Child's Needs

For example, let us say your child is dyslexic. He was not successful in the typical classroom. He struggles to hear the differences in sounds and is not advancing in reading as he should. You decide to go to a tutoring center. They give him instruction one on one but they use the same methods a classroom teacher would use. He will likely do a little better with the one on one and the extra immersion time in reading but will also still be struggling to file and retrieve the information in his brain due to his different learning style. This can frustrate him even more because now he has even less free time. He still has to go home and complete homework that is still difficult to do. His self- esteem is affected because he will think he is not smart enough to learn.

This type of scenario would require you to make a change and quickly. The program needs to match your child's specific needs. I cannot stress that enough. No matter what the advertising says, if it is not working for your child, it is just not working. Make a change.

Example of Instruction Meeting Child's Needs

The program that would suit this child would probably do the following. First, they would interview the child to find out more about him. During this interview they would perform several assessments to discern his current level in all the different areas that feed into the reading process. The tester will compare these scores to the "average" score for this age and grade level. The instructor will then analyze the results of all the tests, and formulate a plan that takes into account this particular child's needs and personality. He will begin the reading plan at the appropriate level based on the assessments. Each lesson will be based on what occurred in the previous lesson. The instructor will be in tune with the child's strengths and weaknesses and adjust each lesson accordingly. The child will be actively engaged during each lesson. This means reading, writing, discussing, demonstrating, manipulating materials, etc. This type of lesson will see dramatic results.

Instructor Needs Explicit Training

Do not expect the tutoring program to be successful just because the tutor is a certified teacher. I made this mistake with my daughter. Teachers are not taught how to teach reading in a general bachelor degree program. My undergrad program only required two classes in reading. This gave me a background in reading instruction but did not teach me how to explicitly teach reading to a child with a learning difference. I believe this instruction should be a mandatory requirement for a reading specialist as well as teachers in kindergarten to third grade.

I received a Master's Degree in Reading but still did not know how to explicitly teach a child with a learning difference how to read. I learned an incredible amount of information concerning reading but nothing about a specific program for children who struggle. The whole reason I wanted to learn about reading was to teach the children who struggle. The other children will learn no matter what you do. The ones who struggle need specific materials and techniques. I believe explicit training in one of the multisensory programs is crucial for a reading specialist to be successful. This training would also be extremely beneficial for Kindergarten through Third grade teachers.

Some people might advocate for the fact that this should be in the realm of the Special Education teacher. I disagree. Many children in the special education classification are only there because they cannot read. This problem will affect all their other course work. They look like they should be placed in special education classes on paper, but in reality, they just need a good intervention program for reading.

University programs do vary from state to state so maybe the teacher you found has a more extensive background in reading but find out for sure. A teacher may go on to acquire additional instruction in this area but it is not mandatory. You have to ask what the instructor's background in reading involves and how much experience they have and in what programs. Do not let your child be the guinea pig for someone experimenting or just learning a program. Make sure you find someone qualified in an explicit multisensory program that is research based and proven effective. This expertise will ensure your child's reading success and in the fastest time possible.

The Difference between a Tutor and a Specific Reading Program Methodology

There is a world of difference between a specific reading program and a tutoring session. An ineffective tutoring session will use worksheets and require your child to read something he cannot read and the tutor will be sounding out the difficult words for him. A specific reading program will be following a sequence based on your child's level at this time. It will use several different formats such as letter cards and word building, sand trays, play dough, and dry erase boards. Your child will be making words, changing words, writing, and reading.

The program will also use what was observed during the lesson to format the next lesson. It will be flexible according to the learner's needs, strengths and weaknesses, but also have a strict sequence of what is to be covered and mastered before going any further. Each program has its own methods but worksheets should not be a big part of the program.

Choice 3 – Implement a Program at Home

I will start with the pros and cons for this choice and then discuss three effective programs a parent can use successfully at home.

Choice 3 - Implement Program at Home
Pros: More affordable
You know and love your child better than anyone else
More convenient
Can be a very rewarding experience for both parent and child
Cons: Lack of experience and training;
Difficult to work with your own child;
More time demands on you;
Can be an excruciating painful experience for both parent and child

Pros of Program at Home

Let's start with the pros. Implementing a reading program yourself can be much more affordable. You only need to pay for the program you are using and some supplies. The cost of this will vary from program to program. This is a one time out of pocket expense and you do not have to pay an hourly wage. The price will range from under $100 dollars to under $1,000 dollars depending on the program and the materials you choose.

The program and materials you choose will depend on the age of your child, the extent of the learning difference, and how much material he needs to cover to catch up to his grade level. All things considered, this is much more affordable than attending a professional program or paying a professional tutor.

I chose option 2 with my daughter. The program cost approximately $20,000 dollars by the time she completed the program. I put this charge on several credit cards and then took out a home equity loan to cover the credit cards. This hurt us financially and took forever to pay off, but eventually we did pay it off. I would do this again if I had to because she needed it, and it worked, and she is now a very successful adult. Many people are not in a position to do this. That is why I wanted to include another option.

You can be successful in this endeavor with the right attitude and the right tools. You also need to have the understanding that if this option turns out to be too stressful for you or your child, or if your child is not advancing, that you will discontinue the program and find a better fit. Remember the bottom line! Always ask yourself, is your child progressing? If not, make a change. Do not waste valuable time on something that is not working.

You Know Your Child Best

Another pro for this choice is that you know and love your child more than anyone else in the world. You want to see him successful more than anyone else. This is a strong incentive which can encourage you to take on this endeavor. You will know when your child has had enough and when you can push forward. You also know how best to encourage him to continue on until he is successful.

Convenient

This option is also more convenient. You don't have to drive anywhere or worry about being on time. You can always adjust your reading time according to your schedule, not someone else's schedule. Your child never has to miss a game or practice because of a reading lesson. This alone solves many potential disagreements or obstacles to success.

Rewarding

Finally, this experience can be a very rewarding experience for you and your child. We live in such a fast paced, hectic world that this is one way to slow things down and spend time together. It is also something you will remember forever (hopefully for positive reasons). The moment you begin to see progress is very special and helps to encourage you both to continue on and achieve more success.

Cons of Program at Home

The first con is that you probably do not have any experience or training in reading instruction. This can be overcome with the correct materials and a very peaceful, positive attitude. You have to promise yourself that you will exercise patience to the extreme. Sometimes this can be very difficult to say the least, especially with your own child (and I know this from painful, personal experience). The Reading Blocks program was developed for the parent with no reading background.

Sometimes it is Difficult to Work with Your Own Child

Next, it can be extremely difficult to work with your own child. Sometimes your personalities just will not allow for you to work together at home. This is normal and is definitely ok. I have five daughters. Two of them had learning disabilities that involved reading. My first daughter completed an outside program. By the time I discovered a learning disability with a younger daughter I had completed a BS in Mathematics and a Master's programs in reading. I also had well over ten years teaching experience and worked with hundreds of students. I thought it was going to be a breeze to teach one small child early reading skills.

Well it wasn't. Our personalities in an instructional setting clashed like you would not believe. I had to walk away a number of times so I would not say what I wanted to say or do what I wanted to do. I had to force myself to give her the same respect and patience I gave to my other students. We were ultimately successful, but it was a major learning experience for me. So whether you have a background in reading or not, a big component of your success will rely on if your personalities are compatible to work this closely together. If you exercise extreme respect and tons of patience, you can be successful.

Puts More Pressure on You

Finally, this choice will put the whole burden of your child's reading success on your shoulders. You will be giving up a lot of your time to learning the program, planning the lessons and then implementing the lessons. While this is very rewarding, it can also be very difficult. You are the only one who can really decide if you are up to the challenge. And of course remember, if it does not work, change it. You are not a failure if you decide it is not working for you. Your goal is your child successfully reading and how you get there is not as important as just getting there.

Three Effective at Home Programs

I have used three programs that I found to be very effective and can be implemented by a parent at home. I like these programs because they all use multisensory methods, are explicit in their instruction, follow a sequential format, are based on methods backed by research, and are easy to follow. The programs are: *Sonday System, Hooked on Phonics*, and the newly released Reading Blocks: A Step by Step Method to Teach Reading.

Each has unique qualities that benefit a range of learning abilities and learning differences, as well as ages. Remember though, each child is different in where they are at, where they need to go, and what type of learning difference is interfering with their progress in reading. Some parents can be very successful at home with their particular situation and others cannot. You have to weigh all the pros and cons of your situation when making this decision.

Each one of these programs is very explicit in directions and format and follows a sequential pattern of instruction. They are all research based and include some multisensory functions. You will have to take a look at each to see which one is best able to meet your child's needs. All three are definitely good for kindergarten to third grade instructional levels and age levels. The *Sonday System* and Reading Blocks: A Step by Step Method to Teach Reading can be used through upper grades and beyond if necessary. The problem with using certain material with an older child is that the reading material is usually suited to a younger reader. The older reader can be embarrassed to be reading "babyish" material. You need to make sure the reading material is age appropriate as well as instructional level appropriate. This can be accomplished with leveled readers that use a controlled vocabulary.

Leveled readers are books written specifically for reading instruction. They contain grammar and vocabulary that starts on a very rudimentary level and systematically increases in difficulty with each additional book. These books are helpful for choosing material at the appropriate level to practice reading skills being taught in a specific lesson. Recommended leveled readers can be found on my website, www.TheReadingTutor.org.

Reading Blocks: A Step by Step Method to Teach Reading

Reading Blocks is a phonics based, multisensory reading system. This system is designed according to the latest research on the most effective way to teach reading. Reading Blocks breaks up the learning to read process into 32 blocks, or chunks of knowledge. Each block contains everything you need to know and use in order to successfully teach that reading block. You will systematically build a reading wall of knowledge, block by block beginning with simple alphabet sounds and ending with decoding advanced sound combinations.

The Reading Blocks manual is designed with a blank back side of all activity pages. This allows you to tear out and cut up the activity page instead of having to make a copy. This manual is meant to be used.

Corresponding videos are also available. Each video follows a reading specialist teaching a reading block. The videos can be used for teaching the block or for review of the block after the initial instruction. Each video can be purchased individually so you only need to download any video that applies to your situation.

Checkpoints are included after every five blocks to make sure that the reader is learning and remembering the information. The checkpoints can also be used when a reader is starting the program at a block other than block one. The checkpoints combine the information from each of the previous five blocks into one assessment and can be used to evaluate whether or not the individual has mastered that material. This ensures that there is no missing information in the readers' knowledge base or wall of knowledge.

Reading Blocks can be used effectively with any learning difference including: Dyslexia, Autism, Aspergers, Downs Syndrome, CAPD, ADD, and ADHD. Reading Blocks includes multisensory activities and controlled vocabulary mini books to practice the new reading skills in each block. This system uses an easy to follow format which does not require months of training and is the most cost effective option.

Reading Blocks requires the use of inexpensive office supplies such as file folder, binder, post-it notes, and colored markers. Leveled Readers are recommended for additional practice using a controlled vocabulary appropriate for each level of reading. One mini book is included in each reading block which uses a controlled vocabulary.

Reading Blocks was designed to be used with all age levels, including adult non-readers. The current price of the Reading Blocks system is $39.95. Each video is available for download for $5.

Sonday Program

The *Sonday* program comes in three levels. The first is called *Let's Play Learn* and is appropriate for preschool through kindergarten. The second level is called the *Sonday System I* and covers instructional material through about the third grade instructional level (not age level). The third level is called the *Sonday System II* and continues from about the third grade instructional level, to about the eighth grade instructional level.

Each level comes in a binder format and includes all the materials needed to complete the instruction. The *Sonday System* also comes with a video or CD training to watch that shows you exactly how to implement the lessons. This program can be learned and implemented by a parent.

The current price of the *Sonday System I and II* is about $450 dollars each. You definitely want to include the *Sonday Readers* if you do this program. They are leveled readers which follow the same skill sequence as in the program and reinforce the skills learned in each lesson. The readers cost about $75 dollars for the set.

The readers are necessary because it is very important for the child to practice the skills he just learned in the lesson with a book format. Regular books do not have the controlled text and can have too many difficult words. This tends to discourage a struggling reader. For example, after you introduce the short /a/ sound, and the consonant sounds of /t, c, p and l/, and a few sight words, you can practice sounding out the phonemes and reading words in a book using the controlled text format. These readers do just that, and each reader shows you the sounds and skills being practiced on the cover.

The readers also use a controlled vocabulary which becomes progressively more difficult as the level increases. The progression matches each of the lesson plans in the program. This makes it much easier to find something to read that matches the reading level of your child. You need to connect the learning of all these random sounds with actual words, then sentences and ultimately stories. These readers are also great to use with any other program.

Hooked On Phonics Program

I think almost everyone is familiar with *Hooked on Phonics*. This program has evolved over the years and has definitely improved. First, it is easy to understand and implement. You do not need any background in teaching or reading instruction to be successful.

Second, each level has all the materials you need to complete that level. There is a lot of repetition, which can sometimes be a little boring for kids, but you can always move on as soon as you feel your child has mastered the skill. This program now uses more multisensory activities than in the original version. You can always intertwine more multisensory activities into this program according to your child's needs. Check the appendix for a list of multisensory activities and resources.

Finally, this program comes with its own books. The books have a controlled vocabulary and controlled sounds that correspond to the material being introduced or reviewed in each reading level.

The *Hooked on Phonics Master Reader Deluxe Edition* currently costs around $159 dollars and covers the instructional levels from kindergarten through second grade. You also have access to additional practice material on the internet with the price of the program. They offer additional programs which you can review on their website. All in all, it's a very user friendly program and can be very successful.

Decision Time

So far you have completed your investigation, you have looked at your options and now you've hopefully decided on a program which you believe is best suited to your child's situation. It is time to begin. For each option (school program, private program, at home program) I will discuss:

- What to do in the beginning of the program.
- What to look for in your child.
- What to look for in the program.
- What does success look like in the program.
- What does lack of success look like in the program.
- What should you be doing at home.

You can skip to the section describing the option you chose or review all sections before making your choice.

Points to Ponder

- You have three choices for implementing a reading program: **School program**; **Private Party program**; **At Home program**. There are pros and cons for each program.
- **School Program Pros**: Less commitment for parent; no extra cost; easiest choice.
- **School Program Cons**: may not match child's specific needs; must accept whatever is offered; may take time away from other subjects.
- **Private Party Pros**: more freedom in choosing specific program; can match program to child's needs; can be more effective and raise reading level quicker than school program.
- **Private Party Cons**: can be costly; can be time consuming; requires more personal commitment; requires research into program credentials.
- **At Home Program Pros**: affordable; you know your child best; you care the most if your child succeeds; convenient; can be rewarding for you and your child.
- **At Home Program Cons**: possible lack of experience and training; difficult to work with your own child; the whole responsibility is on your shoulders.
- A Quality Program Should Be: Researched Based; Multisensory; systematically sequenced; include controlled reading practice; include an assessment component for each level or section; and fit your child's specific needs.
- Most Importantly: You Should See Progress. If not, adjust or change the program.

Chapter 6

Implement and Evaluate School Program

"There is no failure except in no longer trying. There is no defeat, except from within; no really insurmountable barrier save our own inherent weakness of purpose."

Elbert Hubbard

You have completed your investigation. You have looked at your options. And now, you have decided on a program which you believe is best suited to your child's situation. It is time to begin. I will discuss:

- What to do in the beginning of the program.
- What to look for in your child.
- What to look for in the program.
- What success looks like in the program.
- What lack of success looks like in the program.
- What you should be doing at home to ensure success.

Option 1: School Program

What to Do in the Beginning of the Program

You should have been given assessment results which show your child's current level in very specific areas such as letter sound knowledge, phonemic awareness level, decoding level, sight word level, comprehension level, fluency level, vocabulary, and whatever else pertained to your child's unique situation. You want to know your child's current skill level so you can judge the progress being made (or not,) and the effectiveness of the program. You should also have been given the plan of action that the school has agreed to perform to increase your child's reading skills. Both you and your school's team should have agreed on this plan of action.

Remember, all of these decisions must take into account your child's reading level, how far behind he is, and the available resources at his school. The plan of action may include intensive daily pull-out interventions for a child who has a lot of catching up to do or a plan less intensive for someone who is not as far behind. You should have agreed to these interventions during the IEP (Individual Education Plan) meeting. Now it is your job to check that he is receiving these interventions and that they are actually working.

Sometimes, not always, everyone involved can become complacent by thinking that the problem is solved, "Johnny's in a reading program." Nothing is solved yet. There can be holidays, field trips, maternity leaves, fire drills, etc. that interfere with your child's time slot in school. This is no one's fault. It is just a fact.

Monitor Progress

You should find out how your child's progress is being monitored. Will there be an informal reading inventory taken? If so, how often? You want to make sure you are getting all the results. You might not get all the results if you do not ask for them. Will his phonemic awareness skills be checked? If so, how often, and with what tools? You want the results.

Ask for a copy of each assessment as they are completed so you can monitor your child's progress. If you are only seeing progress results once a month, you better be seeing marked improvement scores each time. If there is no improvement, the intervention is **not** working.

The speed of improvement depends on the severity of your child's learning difference of course, but you need to see improvement regularly, not intermittently. You have to be diligent in checking for this improvement. Time goes by fast during the school year and your child will be even farther behind without this progress.

I did not check for progress with my daughter and she was two more years behind because of this oversight. I assumed the school was taking care of her reading problem and I should not have. This was my responsibility as her parent.

This is also just a good double check system for everyone involved. If you are seeing progress each time you check, good keep checking. If you are not seeing progress, ask for a meeting. You want to meet with the child's teacher and the person or persons responsible for the interventions. Ask questions. Find out what could be going wrong. Discuss some changes that can be made. This is especially important in the beginning of the intervention. Once the child and teacher find what works for them both, progress will speed up. Discuss the changes being made and then check that these changes are working.

Keep up a dialogue between you and the child's teacher and the person or persons doing the interventions. There is a better chance for progress when you are following the results closely. The squeaky wheel really does get more attention. Everyone seems to stay more focused when the parent is closely monitoring the results.

If your child's personality clashes with the interventionist, ask if there is someone else that can implement the program with him. If there is no one else to work with your child in this program, you might want to consider another program. Remember, your goal here is for your child to read, not to argue about whether the school is doing their job or not. Sometimes it is just not going to work out in a school setting. You do not want to look back in 18 years when your child is still a non-reader and say it was all the school's fault. It is not the school's fault. It will be yours. So, just bite the bullet here and get the job done, whatever it takes.

What to Look For in Your Child

Is he more confident? Does he read more on his own at home? Will he read with you for fun, not because he is forced? Does he seem happier going to school? Do you personally notice any improvements in his reading skills? You should say yes to all of these questions within a month or two.

You may not see a ton of progress but there should be enough progress to change your child's attitude towards his ability to read. He should at least feel that it is possible for him to be successful in reading. If your child is acting up more or very discouraged something is not working. Make an appointment and find out what is going wrong. It is crucial for your child to see improvement in his skills once the interventions have begun. If he does not see improvement when getting extra help, he will become more negative about himself and his abilities.

This is just another reason why you have to be very diligent in checking for progress in the beginning of the intervention. One month is long enough to see improvements. If none are made, a drastic change is necessary.

What to Look For in the Program

You should know exactly where your child is when beginning the program. For example, if your child is in second grade, I would want to know:

- phonemic awareness level
- letter and sound proficiency
- decoding level
- sight word level
- comprehension level
- fluency level

Each school might offer other additional assessments according to your child's specific needs.

Know all baseline levels and target levels. Next make sure you know when each area is being assessed and with what tool. It may be daily, twice a week, weekly, or every other week depending on what is being assessed. As long as you know when it should be happening, you can be on the look-out for the results. If you do not receive them, ask for them. Make sure you are seeing progress during most intervals. Make sure you are also seeing progress at home. If not, make an appointment and find out why.

What Does Success Look like in this Program

Success is improvement in your child's self-esteem and positive beliefs in his ability to read now or in the near future. He feels like he is "getting it.' That is success. When this happens you will also see his assessment scores go up in each area of assessment. This must happen in a timely manner. You cannot wait two years to see success. You should have little successes continuously along the way, every day, every week, and every month. Chapter 9 gives examples of real life situations of what success and lack of success looks like in this program.

Each success story will be unique but they will have similar threads. Each will have someone who cares enough about the child to put in the extra work. Each will have a sound intervention plan that fits the child's needs. The intervention plan will be monitored consistently for success in meeting the unique needs of this child. Adjustments to the plan will be made in a timely manner which enables the child's skills to continuously move towards the goal.

What Does Lack of Success Look Like in This Program

Lack of success will show in lack of progress. The child will not reach a higher skill level and will become increasingly frustrated with reading and school. Tension may increase at home, especially during homework time. The child will continue to avoid any kind of reading and when he does read, it can be emotional and painful. It will be painful on both the child's end and the parent's end. The child may act out in school or at home. Some children become the class clown or the class antagonist.

I am generalizing here but it is difficult to say because each situation will be unique. Watch your child closely during the intervention time. You will be able to see signs giving you clues as to which way this is headed. You will also be following the assessment results closely which will confirm what you are seeing at home. Any time you are not sure about your child's progress, call the person involved and discuss your concerns.

Each failure story will also be unique but have similar threads. The end result being that the child failed to advance to the level necessary for success. The degree of failure will vary. The situation will vary. But, the ultimate result is the same, below average reading skills.

Do not become discouraged if this happens with you and your child. Life sometimes gets in the way for a myriad of reasons. You must try again. Sit down together and go over what worked, what did not work, and where did the reading plan fail or stop moving forward? Use these answers to formulate your next plan.

Do not give up. You can and will be successful if you keep attacking the situation. Keep motivating your child. Make sure that he continues to believe in his ability to succeed in whatever he chooses. You might choose to try this option again, maybe with a different teacher, or maybe with a different attitude, depending on the situation. You might choose to try another option all together. Just do something positive to move your child forward

What You Should be Doing At Home

You want to reinforce at home what your child is working on during the reading intervention. You want to make this practice more game-like than homework. This practice should be easy for him, not stressful. He has enough stress during the school day. If he is working on alphabet sounds, have alphabet magnets on the refrigerator and on the walls around his bed. If he does not know the sounds yet, just start with a few and as he learns them add more. You can say the alphabet sounds and have him use a pointer and point to the letter that makes that sound. This is easier than pointing to the letter and saying the letter name and the sound by himself. After he masters this skill, move on to the next one.

The car is a great place to practice alphabet sounds and phonemic awareness skills. You have a captive audience while you are all stuck in the car driving. If you make it fun, he will not view it as work. Another great tool is to keep dry erase boards in the back seat for practicing writing the sounds as you say them or as you pass by something. For example, when you pass a restaurant or animal, you can say the word and have him tell you the first sound he hears. Then have him write the letter that makes that sound. As he progresses, he can practice writing the beginning, middle, and last sound, and then the whole word.

You can be very creative and find 10 minute intervals throughout the day. If it feels like a game he will join you. If it feels like something he cannot be successful at, he will not want to join. Bedtime is another very useful time to practice his skills with games. Using the wall space in a room is called passive learning and can be very effective for reinforcing any skill. If he is working on sight words, cut out the words and place them on his bedroom walls and anywhere else he spends time. Practice reading the words before bed. You can make a game of this by saying "I'm thinking of a word that begins with /b/". Then he guesses which word you are thinking of by reading all the "B" words until he guesses the correct word. You can place each word under the corresponding letter of the alphabet which can go around the room.

You can change all of this according to his level and what he needs to learn. Older children can use their time in the car according to what they need. Their wall space can be filled with material they need to learn.

Bedtime reading is also very important. You can read to him or have him read to you. It is best to have a large variety of books at all levels but make sure there are some at his current level. If he is a non-reader make sure to have some alphabet books to expose him to the alphabet sounds in a relaxed environment. Some nights he might prefer to be the reader and if he does not feel like it you can be the reader. Always let him choose the story, of course.

A fabulous book for making learning fun at home, especially for children with learning differences, is called *Word Play* by Lori Goodman and Lora Myers. This is one of my favorite books and includes ABC phonics games, vocabulary and sight word games, comprehension games, prewriting/writing games and more. This book also incorporates multisensory learning which is crucial for children with learning differences and shows you how to incorporate these games into your regular routine. Three other books I have used extensively are: *Learning to Read is Child's Play, Recipe for Reading, and Brain Gym*. Details for each of these books and several more are in the appendix.

Points to Ponder

- Know where your child is and where he needs to go.
- Check for regular assessments.
- Check for continuous progress.
- Develop a good rapport with the teacher implementing the reading program. Contact her if you notice a lack of progress.
- Do you notice your child reading more? Is reading more enjoyable? If not, find out why.
- Is your child's self-esteem high? If not, find out why.
- The squeaky wheel gets the attention. Let everyone know that you are closely monitoring your child's progress.
- Read together every day.
- Be creative in finding small increments of time for fun practice.

Chapter 7

Implement and Evaluate a Private Program

"The secret of all power, all achievement, and all possession, depends upon our method of thinking."

Charles F. Haanel

You have completed your investigation. You have looked at your options. And now, you've decided on a program which you believe is best suited for your child's situation. It is time to begin. I will discuss:

- What to do in the beginning of the program.
- What to look for in your child.
- What to look for in the program.
- What success looks like in the program.
- What lack of success looks like in the program.
- What you should be doing at home.

What to Do in The Beginning of The program

The private program will have a person, or team of people, to complete their own assessment protocol. They will meet with you to discuss your child's skill level and their plan of action for increasing his skills. They will begin their program at the skill level that most accurately corresponds to your child's skill level. They can also incorporate any other assessments that were already performed elsewhere into their plan of action.

You should have a consultation with the supervisor to discuss where your child is at this moment in time, and what the target levels will be for your child. The supervisor will also tell you what assessments will be done along the way to check for progress. He cannot tell you exact times for your child to reach any goals. Each timeline will vary from child to child. He can give you some general guidelines for progress, according to this particular program's average results.

He should also tell you exactly what the program can offer your child and how it will meet your child's specific needs. You and your child should also meet the instructor that will be working with your child. Find out how much experience this instructor has in this particular program. If he is new, does he seem well trained and confident in his ability to work with your child? Does he seem to have a good rapport with your child? You will be paying a lot of money for this instruction and you want to optimize your results.

Two ways to do this are to develop a good rapport with the person working with your child and checking your child's progress consistently. Do not just sit back and hope for the best. Be as actively involved as possible without interfering with their work. When a person who is working with your child knows that you are checking, they will make sure that they are doing their best. You do not want to make enemies here. You just want to hold people accountable to do what they claim they are doing. Some of the programs have a high turnover of employees and you want to make sure you have someone dedicated to your child's success with this program.

Familiarize yourself with the program. Understand the activities which your child will be doing as well as the materials being used. This will help you to more completely understand the progress reports and have a better gauge of the effectiveness of the program up to each checkpoint. This will also help you to communicate with your child about what he is doing in the program. You want to continue to keep him motivated, especially early on in the program.

To recap, when you begin this program, you want to know exactly where your child is and where he needs to be, or his target levels. You want to understand the components of the program and what your child will be doing on a daily basis. You want to develop a good rapport with the instructor so you can freely discuss your child's progress. You want regularly scheduled progress reports, and to actually see progress on these reports. You want to make sure that your child and the instructor have a good working relationship to maximize results.

Finally, you want to closely observe your child for positive results of the program. He might be fighting with you in the beginning because it is very difficult work and he might not want to do the work. But you should start to see his skills improving and that always helps to motivate both of you.

Remember, in the beginning especially, you might have to use some sort of reward system to motivate your child to work hard. This depends on your child's personality but you know better than anyone else what will motivate him. Rewards make the process easier to swallow for everyone.

What to Look For in Your Child

Is he more confident? Does he read more on his own at home? Will he read with you for fun, not because he is forced? Does he seem happier going to school? Do you personally notice any improvements in his reading skills? You should say yes to all of these questions within a month or two. You may not see a ton of progress but there should be enough progress to change your child's attitude towards his ability to read. He should at least feel that it is possible for him to be successful in reading.

If your child is acting up more or very discouraged, something is not working. Make an appointment and find out what is going wrong. It is crucial for your child to see improvement in his skills once the interventions have begun. If he does notice improvement when getting extra help, he will become more negative about himself and his abilities.

This is just another reason why you have to be very diligent in checking for progress in the beginning of the intervention. A couple of weeks should be enough time to see improvements. If none are made, a change is necessary. Find out if the problem lies with the program, the person implementing the program, or an issue with your child. In the private setting you have more freedom to make adjustments.

Does your child seem to be working amicably with the instructor? If not, you can ask for a change in instructors. The program supervisor should be looking out for this also and should recommend a change if there is a personality clash. This does not happen too often, but it does happen. You should be aware of this and be ready to ask for a change if necessary.

Is your child happy enough to be going to this program? There can be some resistance because it is such difficult work but it should not be an extreme sport to get him there. If he is always very upset about attending this reading program, and it is very difficult for you to get him to go, then you might need to make adjustments. Either the motivator you are using or possibly the program itself is not working. He will not reach his full potential if he hates it. You will have to decide in this situation if the program is not a good fit for him or if you can find a way to motivate him with something he really wants.

Always look for subtle clues in his actions about how he is doing. You will be able to tell when the session is positive and when it has been a negative experience. Try to hold a discussion after each session to uncover any warning flags, so a change can be made before too much time has passed. This is easy to say but sometimes very difficult to do. Many boys would rather do just about anything else on this earth than carry on a discussion about school, or just a discussion, period. The girls will talk, talk, and talk some more about every minute detail of the day. That is, until they reach a certain age, and then all of a sudden, they despise you and your stinking discussion. So just do your best and look for the subtle clues if you are not dealing with a great communicator. You know your child and you will know what to look for when he is experiencing success and when he is feeling like a failure.

What to Look for in The Program

Is this program meeting your child's specific needs? Does it seem like a good fit with your child? Are your child's reading skills improving? Does your child like the program, or at least, not hate it? Are the supervisor and instructor(s) easy to talk to and open about sharing your child's progress? Are they professional and kind, especially to your child? They are working for you, not the other way around. You should feel comfortable discussing your child's progress with them and not feel like you are bothering them.

The bottom line here, is the program working for your child? You should have a good idea within a month. If you are having problems, discuss them with the supervisor or instructor. Can adjustments be made that suit all concerned, but especially to suit your child's needs? If the program does not seem to work for your child's situation, find another one that does. Do not waste too much time if it is just not working out. You want to give the program a chance but not waste a lot of time if it is not a good fit.

As with all the other programs, you want to know exactly where your child's skill levels are in the beginning and where he needs to go, or target levels. You want to make sure you are consistently checking for progress with predetermined progress checkpoints. You want to keep a good rapport with the instructor so you can discuss any difficulties and make adjustments along the way. Most programs can be adjusted in some way to fit the individuality of each child. Make sure you are seeing progress along the way at each checkpoint and if not, discuss the necessary changes.

What Success Looks Like in the Program

Success looks the same in this program as all the others, improvement in your child's actual reading ability, as well as improvement in his beliefs about his reading ability. His self-esteem should be increasing. He should feel like he is "getting it". That is success.

When this occurs you will begin to see his assessment scores start to climb. When the scores are graphed, the trend should be rising. There can be ups and downs as long as the general trend keeps going up. If not, something needs to be changed. Every child is unique and his learning patterns will be unique also. Adjustments always need to be made to improve the fit between the instruction and the child's needs. Chapter 9 relays a real life story of success using this option, as well as a story of failure in this option.

What Lack of Success Looks Like In the Program

Lack of success will show in lack of progress. You should see progress within a couple of weeks of beginning the program if the program is working. If you are not seeing progress at home, find out why. Talk to the instructor and the supervisor. Does your child get along with the instructor? Is the program a good fit for the learning difference? Is your child sufficiently motivated to put in the extra effort it will take to be successful? Look at all these situations and make any necessary changes. If the program just is not working for your child, then you will have to find another one that will. As with the other programs, look for telltale signs in your child's behavior. You will be able to see a difference when the program is effective. If you are seeing no changes, the program is not working.

I have personally found *Wilson, Lindamood-Bell, Reading Blocks: A Step by Step Method to Teach Reading, Sonday System*, and *Hooked on Phonics* to be successful for various levels of severity in reading difficulties. Most programs based on Orton-Gillingham research and multisensory methods should also be effective. Orton-Gillingham is a method of teaching reading based on research and practice by Samuel Orton and Anna Gillingham. Dr. Orton connected language processing difficulties with reading failure and studied how to best work with these children. Anna Gillingham worked with Dr. Orton and developed a structured program for others to use. Programs based on their research and methods are extremely effective.

The Irlen method of using colored overlays definitely can be very effective for some children and can be used in addition to one on one instruction with a multisensory program. Your program and whatever at-home tools you use will depend on the severity of your child's reading difficulty, as well as his personal and unique needs. Check the appendix for a listing of some of the effective products for at-home use backed by research and results. You might want to incorporate one into your child's program or use after completion of a program, for extra support.

What You Should Be Doing At Home

No matter which program you use, you should always be encouraging, praising, and supporting your child's efforts. Always keep building their self-esteem at this time because usually it is low. Also, use whatever you can to motivate your child to work as hard as possible during this time. As I said before, it is very hard work for them and some kind of compensation works wonders.

You might also want to adjust some of the homework requirements if the reading program is intense. You will have to discuss this with his teacher so there is no trouble at school. You do not want to overwhelm your child during this time and sometimes this involves skipping something else. Right now, learning to read is the most important issue in his life. Almost everything else comes after this.

Some of the programs provide material for you to practice at home in between sessions. Try and make this practice a game and not drudgery. Depending on the child's age and difficulty, you might be able to do extra practice in the car or while watching a sibling's game. For example, you can practice rhyming or beginning sounds with a kindergarten child anywhere you go. You do not need any tools for this kind of practice. An older child could practice pulling apart and blending the sounds in words you say out loud. A first or second grade child could read aloud to you in the car while you are driving back and forth to appointments or games.

A very important habit for all children to develop is to read each night before bed. You can put a basket of books by each child's bed that contains a variety of books at their interest level and reading ability level. A book can be chosen from this basket each night for you or your child to read aloud. Even 15 minutes a night will make a big difference in your child's reading skills. The teacher or supervisor in your program can offer recommendations for you which take into account your child's unique situation, the program being used, and the elements being learned at that time.

Points to Ponder

- Know where the child's skill levels are and where they need to be.
- Check for progress on a regular basis.
- Develop a good rapport with the person implementing the program.
- You should be noticing improvements in your child's skills.
- You should be seeing your child read more.
- Read daily with your child.
- Provide reading books and materials around your home.
- Remember to: Motivate, Encourage, Praise and Reward.

Chapter 8

Implement and Evaluate At-Home Program

"Every thought therefore is a cause and every condition an effect; for this reason it is absolutely essential that you control your thoughts so as to bring forth only desirable conditions."

Charles F. Haanel

You have completed your investigation. You have looked at your options. And now, you've decided on a program which you believe is best suited to your child's situation. It is time to begin. I will discuss:

- What to do in the beginning of the program.
- How to choose your at-home program.
- What to look for in your child.
- What to look for in the program.
- What success looks like in the program.
- What lack of success looks like in the program.
- What you should be doing at home.

What to Do in the Beginning of the Program

The first step in this program is to know where you are starting from and where you need to go. You need to know the reading skills your child has mastered and the ones he still needs to improve. You are going to rely on the mastered skills to provide the scaffolding for building upon the skills which are lacking. You should be able to get testing completed by the public school in your area, even if your child is not enrolled in that school.

You should get a complete evaluation for three reasons. First, the evaluation might highlight a learning problem that you will want to know about. This information will affect your approach to instruction. Second, it will give you a wealth of information about your child's learning patterns that you can use when planning the instruction. This evaluation will not cost you anything and can be very informative. Third, the testing might uncover information that is helpful for success in other areas of academics.

This information is not mandatory for success but is always very helpful and informative. You will use this information to help plan your instruction. You need to know where your child is in regards to skill level in order to know what you need to teach and where you want to end up.

I had no idea my daughter had a visual perception problem. I never would have learned that if I did not have her evaluated. We were successful in our reading program without this information, but I would have done some things differently had I known. Also, her visual perception difficulty explained her difficulty in mathematics. Now we can apply this knowledge to her mathematics instructional methods.

How to Choose Your At-Home Program

Next, you will need to choose the reading program to follow in your reading intervention. First I will give some guidelines as to which program will best suit certain age groups, and then I will give information about each particular program. You can choose the program that seems to best suit your child's age, skill level, learning difference, and personality. There is a more detailed description of each program in Chapter 12.

Something to remember at this point is that the child's reading level does not have to correspond to the child's age or grade level. A child can be in Third grade and have a reading level at the Kindergarten level. This is not uncommon. When choosing a program you have to consider the age level of the child as well as the reading level. Some programs are better suited for the Kindergarten level and would be too embarrassing for the older child to use even though the material is at his reading level. You need to be sensitive to these issues. You should always strive to encourage and motivate the child and not humiliate or embarrass him with an ill-fitting intervention program.

Reading Blocks: A Step by Step Method to Teach Reading is recommended for all age groups as well as for readers with and without learning differences. Reading Blocks combines literacy research and brain research with common, inexpensive office supplies, and explicit instructions to form a unique and powerful reading program.

Video lessons are also available and can be purchased separately or as a whole. Each video corresponds to one Reading Block. The videos can be used for introducing and teaching each individual block or for extra practice after the block has been introduced. The expense is minimal and you only purchase the blocks that correspond to your reader's individual needs.

For reading levels of first grade to third grade, and ages seven to approximately twelve, I recommend using the *Sonday System I*. For reading levels of third grade and above, and ages nine and above, I recommend the *Sonday System II*. Remember, *Sonday System I* is for reading levels k-3, not grade or age levels. If a child is in sixth grade, but reading at a second grade level, he will have to begin with *Sonday System I*. When he successfully completes this program, he will move on to the next level, the *Sonday System II*.

Hooked on Phonics is also a good program to use at home by parents and I recommend this program for reading levels kindergarten to third grade and ages six to nine.

If your child is in fourth grade or above, and reading more than one year below age level, I recommend that you seek professional reading intervention for your child. You can be successful with Reading Blocks: A Step by Step Method to Teach Reading or the *Sonday System I* and *II*, and can give this a try if you feel strongly about completing this at home, but you need to be very careful about observing your child's progress. You do not want to hold them back any longer. If you try the program and they are not advancing, pursue an outside reading intervention program. It is imperative that your child learn to read as soon as possible.

These are just guidelines. If your child is comfortable with a program and you think it is a good fit, then by all means try that program. Chapter 9 gives real life situations of children who were successful in each of these three programs. These stories are meant to help you analyze your own situation and help you to be aware of some potential problem areas.

What to Look For in the Child

Is he more confident? Does he read more on his own at home? Will he read with you for fun, not because he is forced? Does he seem happier going to school? Are you noticing improvements during the lesson? You should be saying yes to all these questions within a few weeks to a month of starting the program. If not, you will have to uncover what is not working and try to change it. Working with your own child has its own set of challenges and rewards. You have to be diligent in observing the effects of the program and how you are implementing the program. If you are not seeing any progress, reevaluate. You may have to choose another option. Give yourself and your child enough time to adjust to working together, but just be aware that you do not want to waste time if this choice is not working for your child.

Your child should feel successful. He should be comfortable doing the program. The program should not be too difficult or too easy for him. He should not be upset or stressed out during the program. He should be actively participating and somewhat happy. He needs to see that he can be successful in reading. He should also be adequately motivated to work his hardest.

In summary, if your child is progressing and you are still able to keep your sanity and composure, then congratulations! Keep up the good work. On the other hand, if your child is stressed out, you are stressed out, and there is no noticeable improvement in your child's reading skills, then it is time to make a change.

What to Look For in the Program

The program needs to be a perfect fit for your child's needs. You need to know your child's strengths and weaknesses when beginning the program as well as how the program will meet these needs. Does the program fit your child's mental age? Does the program fit your child's reading level? Does it feel too old or too young for him? Is he embarrassed to do this program? He must be comfortable with the fit of this program to his abilities for him to be successful.

The program should have periodic assessment checks to make sure that you are actually progressing. You can also add your own checks at the end of each session. For example, if you are working on learning the sounds for s, p, t, and a. Have these letters written on cards or have letter tiles. Do a quick check at the end of this session and then again at the beginning of the next session that your child knows these sounds. If not, plan on re-teaching these sounds during the next session. Each program should have details for this type of assessment.

Does the program have appropriate reading material? If not, you will have to provide it. There are many good resources in the appendix for this material. You need to tie in any skill you are working on with an appropriate book for practice. Everything your child learns should be directly tied to reading in a book format. He is learning this information in order to read books and he needs to make the transition from skill practice to reading in book form. This should occur during every session.

You will know if the program is not a good fit after a few weeks. You should be seeing noticeable improvements by then. If not, something needs to be adjusted or changed.

What Does Success Look Like in the Program?

Success will be an increase in your child's ability and self-esteem. He should see improvements in his ability to read. He should be more confident about reading. Reading homework should not be a complete nightmare. Reading time should be peaceful and enjoyable, not a crying, screaming session. Your child should continue to advance successfully through the levels of the program. Some days will be more difficult than others but the trend should be upwards.

What Does Lack of Success Look Like in the Program

Lack of success is little or no improvement. Lack of success is also bad attitudes all around. If you dread every session, and your child dreads every session, then something is not working. If you both would rather go to the dentist than do reading together, then something is wrong. If you and your child are not talking to each other, then something is wrong. You need to make a change. This does not mean that you have to quit working together at home. You might need to adjust the length of the lesson or the amount of the material you are using. You might need to do only half of the lesson instead of trying to squeeze in the whole lesson. Maybe you need to look at your motivating system or your prizes. Maybe your reading material is boring. Take a look at what you are doing and see if you can make improvements somewhere. You will know if you are able to do the program together or not. Just be honest with yourself if this choice is not working out. You are not a failure if you cannot do the program at home. At least you tried. It is more important that your child learns how to read than how it occurs.

What Should You Be Doing at Home?

Motivating, praising, rewarding, encouraging. These are all necessary components for success at home. You want to keep your child's self-esteem at a high level. You want your child to feel successful and confident in his abilities. You want him to be happy not miserable. You have to be careful when working at home that you do not overdo the lessons or underdo the lessons. You also want to reinforce what he is learning on a daily basis by innocently placing reading material throughout the house and car. This way you can fit in 10 minute reviews wherever you are.

You can have books, dry erase boards, markers, and flash cards in the car. You can use these in small increments during a drive and in a game format. You can have letters and sight words on the refrigerator and on the bedroom walls. Your child can make words and sentences using magnetic tiles while you make dinner. You can have a basket of books next to his bed. These can be books he is able to sound out as well as beautiful picture books or books on a topic of his choice. You want to build up his endurance to read and this means daily reading. You can also read a story to him every night. Eventually, he will want to do the reading when he is progressing.

The key to success at home is to not make reading a negative chore or an argument. There should be fun involved. Several mini reading reviews during the day is far easier to accomplish than one long, difficult session. Begin your program with short sessions and gradually increase the length. Your child will build stamina for the session as well as for reading.

Motivation is also a key to success. A motivational technique I like to use is to have the child pick out a colored index card. After we complete a lesson, the child can pick a sticker to place on his card. He can use this card to go shopping once a week in a treasure chest. The treasure chest has prizes of all different values from one sticker to ten stickers. The child can keep the card in his practice folder or you can hold on to it. You can also use tickets for shopping. The child receives a set amount of tickets after each session. I always give extra tickets periodically when the child works extra hard. The child can use the tickets for "buying" prizes in the treasure chest. The prizes can be adjusted according to age levels and motivation factor.

When I use this system in the schools, the children receive a ticket after each lesson in which they work hard. They also receive an extra ticket for bringing back something signed or doing extra reading at home. The tickets are kept in their homework folders and paper-clipped to the folder. At the beginning of a new session, I let everyone browse through my treasure chest and see the prizes I have, as well as how much they "cost". This always gives the children incentive to work hard to earn tickets and buy prizes.

One year I had to stamp the back of all my tickets because one student actually bought the same tickets at the dollar store and was "shopping" in my treasure chest almost every day. He finally admitted to buying his own roll of tickets. I must admit that it was pretty creative for a first grader, but not exactly the result I was trying to achieve with my motivation system.

The children love this system and actually do work a lot harder knowing they can go "shopping" for rewards.

Points to Ponder

Components of Success in Any Program

- Program matches child's specific needs.
- Program is adjusted when necessary to fit child's specific needs.
- You are seeing progress.
- Your child is seeing progress.
- Your child is happy and motivated to work hard.
- Your child is reading more on his own.

Things to Do At Home

- Reward   Motivate   Read   Encourage
- Praise   Have plenty of books around the house at your child's reading level and interest level.
- Set aside time every day to read together.
- Post letters, sight words, vocabulary words, and spelling words around the house.
- Be creative in finding small increments of time to practice skills.

Chapter 9

Stories of Success

"Adversity has the effect of drawing out strengths and qualities of a man that would have lain dormant in its absence."
                                                                    Herodotos, Quoted by Brian Tracy in Goals

Anna

This is Anna's reading story. Anna's grandmother, Fiona, asked me to evaluate Anna's reading skills after watching her granddaughter struggle with reading in kindergarten and first grade. Fiona had full custody of Anna. She was especially worried because her own daughter, Anna's mother, had always struggled with reading and it had impacted her life in a very negative way. Fiona did not want to repeat this scenario with her granddaughter.

Anna's test results showed that she was having difficulty with kindergarten level reading material even though she was going into second grade. Anna was obviously a very intelligent little girl and her struggle with reading was taking a toll on her self-esteem. Her grades were becoming progressively worse, as was her disposition at home. They were beginning to disagree on every little detail in their lives and the tension was reaching an unbearable level. Fiona was afraid she was not equipped to handle a young child at this point in her life but there was no other feasible option. This situation needed to work for both of them.

I agreed to work with Anna over the summer. Anna needed to fill in many gaps in her knowledge of sounds and phonemic awareness. She needed specific strategies for sounding out unknown words and a larger sight word base. She desperately needed to feel more confident in her abilities. We began our tutoring with *the Reading Reflex* program. We used the Fry sight word list and began compiling a pile of known words and another pile of unknown words. We used both in different projects and games. We met three days a week over the summer for about 45 minutes a session. We always ended the session reading a text that was at her level. She took home a folder with reading material that was also at her level so she could practice independently at home.

As she became more confident, she read more at home without her grandmother's "nagging." She became much more involved and animated during our sessions. By the end of the summer, she had made remarkable improvement but still needed more instruction, as well as support, to keep from losing her gains. Since they lived too far to receive tutoring over the school year, Fiona and I worked with the school team to develop an intervention program at school.

An IEP meeting took place to address Anna's needs and to put a plan in place at her school. Fiona was ready for the meeting. She had all Anna's scores from the tutoring session. She knew where Anna was and where she needed to go. She was a very active participant in deciding on the plan of action to take place at her granddaughter's school. She closely monitored Anna's progress.

Anna saw the Title I reading instructor every day at first and then the sessions gradually decreased as her skills increased. Fiona consistently monitored what the school was providing and held regular meetings with the intervention teacher. Before each meeting, Fiona would call me and we would discuss where Anna was in her skills and what was needed for the next session. By the end of the school year Anna was at grade level in reading and was no longer receiving reading intervention sessions.

Anna and Fiona still had personality clashes but the tension improved and their home became calm. Their relationship became very strong over this period and Anna went on to be very successful in her education.

This story could have had a very different ending. There are many children just like Anna whose outcome is just the opposite. Anna's outcome was so positive because she had someone close to her who cared enough to make sure that she received the help she needed. Anna began her intervention with a tutor but her school team completed the majority of the interventions. This was a successful situation because Anna's grandmother insisted on being involved in each step of the intervention process. She wanted to know what was going on and went out of her way to ensure her granddaughter received the intervention that worked for her. Presently, Anna is on the honor role in high school. Her future is very bright because her grandmother took the time out of her busy life to do whatever it took to help her granddaughter learn how to read.

Caitlin

I knew my daughter was having trouble learning to read. I suspected there was something wrong when she was around four but since I had no background, and was not an expert, I thought it would be worked out in kindergarten. It was not. Her kindergarten teacher was wonderful and very kind to my daughter but nothing she did was effective for my daughter. This was because she was not trained to teach reading to a child with a severe learning difference. This was not her fault, of course. This type of training is not required for regular classroom teachers.

My daughter could not learn the letter names or sounds. She could not read simple sight words from day to day. One day she would know a sight word or a letter sound and the next day she would not. She could read a word in one sentence but in the very next sentence she would not know the exact same word. She also mixed up the syllables in multisyllabic words. For example, she might say, "mazagine" for magazine. She could not make the two sounds in blends and would pronounce only one of the sounds. For example, she would say "bizgetti" for spaghetti.

Her kindergarten teacher recommended holding her back a year so she would be more "mature." I held her back and the next year she went back to kindergarten with her younger sister who was entering for the first time. She could not absorb the material this time either, only now she had a little sister who was passing her up in reading. Obviously, this caused additional problems and tensions at home. The material was taught the same way it was taught the first time. She could not get it then and she could not get it now.

One day she came home crying. She did not want to talk about it but finally told me what happened at school that day. There was a toy ball in the classroom that you could ask questions to and it would give an answer. My daughter was watching another child while he was playing with the ball. The child then asked the ball if my daughter was the most "stupidest" kid in the classroom and the ball answered "yes." She felt so embarrassed and did not want to go to school anymore. This episode was heartbreaking for both of us, but is not unusual. It is just a fact that kids can say mean things, whether it is intentional or not.

During the second year in kindergarten, her teacher recommended testing for learning disabilities. Since my daughter was in a private school, we had to start the process with our local public school. There was a lot of paperwork to complete, and several appointments for the assessments to be completed with various school personnel, and then a meeting was called. This was my first IEP meeting (Individualized Education Program). This is where they told me for the first time that my daughter had a severe learning difference. They suggested that she see the school psychologist for poor self-esteem issues and a special education teacher for additional help with reading skills. They recommended pulling her out of the private school and placing her in a special education classroom at the public school. They also recommended medicine for ADD.

I did not agree with these recommendations. I knew she was smart. She just could not learn how to read. This was impacting her learning levels in several areas. Her inability to read was also impacting her scores on the tests they had given her. This issue was definitely impacting her self-esteem. As far as the ADD, I instinctively knew that any child who could sit through a 3 hour movie without flinching could not possibly have ADD. She could remember every minute detail as well. I knew her main issue was the reading problem. I knew I had to address this issue but I did not know how.

Since I did not know any better at this time, I assumed the school would be able to address her reading issue. We agreed on after school sessions because I did not want to pull her out of the classroom during the regular school day, and have her bussed to the public school for her reading interventions. I picked her up after her full day of school and drove to the next school. Then I and her two sisters waited in the car for the hour and a half, and then went home. Then at home, we began the nightly struggle with completing her reading assignments and homework for school. She would get so frustrated and angry when trying to read an assignment that she would throw the book across the room. Homework was always extremely difficult and stressful for the whole household. This went on for around two years.

Looking back, I wonder why I waited so long. But I think the reason was that I thought they were the experts and I was not qualified enough to make the necessary changes. I thought they could help her and I knew I could not. Also, I would see some progress and hope that this was the start of her full reading "recovery", but then it would not last or would not be substantial enough. Regardless of what I thought, the truth was that she was falling farther and farther behind in her reading skills. This plan of action was not working.

One day I went in early to pick her up from the special education teacher's room during her after school session and found her under the table. The teacher was working with two other students while my daughter just sat under the table. I asked the teacher why my daughter was under the table. She replied that my daughter did not want to do any work today so they agreed she would just sit under the table. I discussed this with my daughter and discovered that the teacher just gave her answers to homework during these sessions. My daughter was frustrated that this was not helping her learn how to read. She felt it was a waste of time and she hated going. Now she was at the end of second grade and she was still way behind in reading. I decided that day that I was quitting all the "extra help" at the public school and would find something on my own.

I started looking into testing outside of the school district. I finally began to get some answers after having my daughter evaluated by an audiologist. She was diagnosed with severe CAPD (Central Auditory Processing Disability) that affected three areas of her brain. The audiologist explained that my daughter could hear the sounds coming in just fine. The trouble began when the sound went from the ear canal to the brain. Information would become "mixed up" in the brain. My daughter would then have trouble "finding" or retrieving this information. This resulted in mixed up syllables in words, transposing words and numbers, and a slew of other manifestations. The audiologist gave me several recommendations including specific strategies to improve her filing and retrieval of information in her brain. These skills would also help to improve her reading skills. She also recommended a reading program that would address these specific issues.

I brought this information to her classroom teacher at the private school and she recommended I take her out of the private school and place her in a special education classes full time at the public school. According to her, their school was not equipped to handle learning differences of this nature. I wanted to keep her in the same school as her sisters. I did not feel she needed special education classes. She just needed to learn how to read. She was very smart in so many ways and very confident at home. I believed all her difficulties lied in the fact that she could not read.

It was right after this that I attended my last IEP meeting for this child. This was one of the most painful meetings I have ever attended. I had to sit and listen to opinions about my daughter and her skill levels that I did not agree with. I felt like such a dummy because I did not graduate from college at this time and I once again assumed they were all experts. After one final remark from a very arrogant participant, I mustered enough courage to ask if she had any experience with CAPD. This person did not. Then I asked if she knew what CAPD was. She did not. I asked if anyone in this room was familiar with CAPD. Not one of them was familiar with this learning difference. Finally, I asked them how they expected to work with my daughter when they knew nothing about her specific learning difference or effective strategies that would work for her. I decided during this meeting that I would discontinue any services being offered from this source.

This process took two years. I should have been more confident in my own judgment concerning my own daughter. Now please do not get me wrong here. Most school districts and IEP teams will not look like this. I just share this with you so that you will be prepared to speak up for your child's needs if they are not being met by your school. Whether you have a degree or not is irrelevant. You know your child and you will be able to tell if he is progressing or not. If he is not progressing, do not waste your time arguing with anyone. If the school cannot meet your child's needs, find another program outside of school that will meet your child's needs. It may be expensive and time consuming but it does not last forever. Before you know it, the program will be over and you will not only have a child who can read, you will have a child whose odds of being successful have just soared. My daughter's story continues and ends in success.

Caitlin was diagnosed with CAPD (Central Auditory Processing Disorder) by an audiologist. The audiologist recommended a program called Lindamood-Bell. I went to an introductory presentation to learn more about this program. I heard many stories of children with learning differences that successfully overcame their learning challenges using this program. Many of the stories were very similar to my daughter's situation. I thought it was definitely worth a try. I called the local branch and set up an appointment to have my daughter assessed by their personnel.

Next, Caitlin was evaluated using several assessments. I met with the director of the program after the testing. She explained what the results meant and which areas of the Lindamood-Bell program would fit Caitlin's needs. She gave me several options for implementing the program which included part time and full time options. Caitlin's assessment uncovered the fact that she was reading at a first grade level and she was now in the beginning of fourth grade at school. This was devastating news to both of us. We were both working so hard to rectify this situation but getting nowhere. After hearing this news, I decided to put her into the program full time. I wanted to take the quickest option possible for bringing her up to grade level and she agreed.

I decided to pull her out of her regular school for this period. I discussed this with the principal at her school and the classroom teacher and they were both very supportive of this decision. She would be in this intensive reading program full time for 12 weeks. I did not want her to have to worry about completing any regular school work at this time. Luckily, they both agreed with me.

Caitlin attended the program from nine to two, five days a week. The nearest facility was an hour drive away, so we drove for 2 hours every day just to attend the program. There were "bumps" along the way during this period. This was extremely difficult work for Caitlin and it was very intense. She had to work on reading for five hours a day, five days a week and then read at home as well. Now remember, this was her weakest area. Reading was the last thing she wanted to do on any given day. Now she was stuck doing only reading all day long. I motivated her to work hard by offering horseback riding lessons. I knew she needed to be positive about the whole experience to achieve the highest level of success. The only way to achieve that was to offer the lessons. She loved horses as much as she hated reading. This did work to motivate her.

The next 12 weeks were difficult to say the least. The time commitment was huge. The expense outlay was huge. The bribery factor was even expensive. But it was worth all the trouble. She went back to her classroom reading at the fourth grade level. Her grades rose. Her self-esteem at school rose. Homework was no longer a nightmare, (well, most nights anyway.) She still has a learning difference but now she is aware of it and finds ways to compensate. She learns differently and always will, but now we know this is an asset, not a disability. This fact does not damage her self-esteem, it actually raises it. Your perception of any situation will be a huge determining factor in your outcome. Having a positive perception definitely increases your success.

Caitlin was very successful in college. She was involved on campus and was elected student class president. Caitlin graduated from college with a double major and even gave the Commencement speech at graduation. We were given special seats to sit in during the graduation ceremony. This was the same little girl whom I was told should be placed in special needs classes. She went on to complete her BSN in nursing and plans on continuing her education in an advanced field in medicine. None of this would have been possible if she could not read. She could possibly still have been successful, but her options would have been much more limited.

A reading disability is NOT a lack of intelligence. It's only a learning difference. We need to find out how each child learns best and then provide this learning platform for them. All children do not learn the same way. They never will and nor should they. Helping our children reach their highest potential is our ultimate goal. This will be achieved by first finding out how they learn best and providing this platform for them.

Michael

First, let me introduce you to our learner. Michael was adopted from China when he was three years old. He was born with a large tumor in his mouth. As he grew, the tumor grew. He was brought to a hospital for surgery by a parent, but then abandoned at the hospital. The surgery was not completely successful. Several facial nerves were severed during the surgery which left half of his tongue paralyzed and half of his face slightly drooped. The doctors were not able to remove the whole tumor and it will grow again as he grows. The paralysis of half of his tongue makes it difficult for him to articulate sounds.

Michael's preschool offered Kindergarten so he stayed at the preschool. This was about the time his mother noticed that he was having difficulty memorizing the alphabet letters and sounds. Since he had a difficult time articulating sounds anyways, his mother was not sure if this was cause for concern or not. Also, his mother was more concerned right now with the social aspect of school and was not worried about letters and sounds. She wanted him to fit in with the other kids and have friends. She thought the letter/sound knowledge would develop as he grew older, but it did not.

First grade came around and his difficulty with reading was more pronounced. His mother decided to place him in a before school reading program with his sister. The program was held from seven to eight AM, before school. He had to get up at 5:30 AM to make it to the program on time. Michael went to this program five days a week for first and second grade.

The program used a computer format and offered a systematic approach to learning letter names, sounds, words, and then sentences. Each child sat at their own computer and completed a lesson based on their level of skill. The program would then give a print out of the progress for the day. There was one person in charge of all the students in this program. This person would set them up at the computer and print out their results for the day.

This program did not include any one-on-one assistance and was not research based. While it may have been suitable for some learners, it was not suitable for Michael's needs. Michael's mother heard testimonials from other parents who raved about their children's results, so she thought it was worth trying. The program did advance her other two children's skills because they did not have specific learning needs like Michael.

On paper, Michael seemed to improve slightly, but he was still having trouble with reading in school and his grades were not strong. His speech was also not improving. He tended to murmur or blur the sounds together making it hard to understand what he was trying to say. Now he was at the end of second grade and falling further and further behind. He wanted to learn and worked hard at learning but was not making substantial progress.

This program was unsuccessful for Michael for several reasons:

- The program did not take into account the learning difference of his facial and tongue paralysis.
- The program did not have one-on-one instruction that he desperately needed.
- The program was not research based and never proven effective. Therefore, it was not a good fit for a child with a learning difference.
- The program did not incorporate any multisensory or hands on components into its structure. These would have helped to reinforce the memory process.

First, and most importantly, the program did not meet Michael's particular needs. The great reviews from others did not take into account the learning differences between the children involved. Michael could not articulate sounds because of the paralysis in his tongue. Many of the alphabet sounds have subtle but very important differences. Michael needed to hear these differences and then practice duplicating them. This process was not occurring in this particular program. He was just randomly guessing at answers on the computer until he found the correct choice. He was connecting the wrong sounds to letters in his head while doing this.

He was also incorrectly learning the sight words. He was connecting the wrong word to a particular stream of letters. This was having a negative impact on his comprehension. Since he was working on his own, no one was correcting these mishaps as they occurred. The computer program did not include one-on-one instruction. No one was checking how he was making the sounds and what sounds he was actually placing on letters. He would say "Uh" for (a), (the) and (of). No one corrected him, so this became a deeply entrenched habit. This is just one example of the many, many different habits he acquired during this period that had to be corrected. As we all know, correcting a long standing habit can be troublesome.

Another growing problem was vocabulary. Since he was misreading words, he was forming his own version of what was happening in the story. This affected his comprehension which in turn affected his vocabulary. He would give his own meanings to words based on his version of the story. Eventually, since most of the story was not making any sense anyways, he just started skipping any word that was challenging to read.

These issues permeated his classroom experience also during this period. Michael found that if he blurred and murmured the sounds, people wouldn't question him. This helped him to camouflage the fact that he could not read. The people working with him were not experienced with the mechanics and intricacies of speech development with partial facial paralysis. They did not want to insult him or act like they were treating him any differently because of his differences. They could not really understand what he said but it sounded close enough so they just let it go.

This was not anyone's fault. His teachers were trying very hard to adjust in the classroom for his learning differences. They did not have the time or the background to address these issues. His school did not have a resource department for children with learning differences or a speech therapist. Michael's story continues with much more positive results.

When we began the Sonday System reading program Michael was nine years old and beginning third grade. Testing revealed that he was reading at a primer level which is still a kindergarten level. He was blurring the sounds for the consonants and just randomly making sounds for the vowel sounds. He did not try to decode words. If he did not know the word outright, he just skipped it. His comprehension was good when the material was read to him. Comprehension was poor when he read the material by himself. This was primarily due to a problem with his decoding and not his actual comprehension. His sight word level was also at the primer level. His fluency was extremely slow.

His main learning differences at this time concerned his speech and reading level. His reading skills suffered because his speech could not be understood and consequently, his erroneous reading patterns were not corrected in a timely manner. One small example of his reading miscues involved the words (a) and (the). The words (a) and (the) are made in the front of the mouth and sound somewhat alike. They both use similar mouth movements but different tongue placement. He was not moving his tongue for these words. When he came across one of these words he would say either word. He was never corrected when he said (the) for (a) or (a) for (the). Since he never had one on one instruction, this error was never corrected, and as a consequence, he interchanged these two words when reading.

There were numerous other instances of this type of error which were never corrected due to his speech difference. Any sounds made in the same mouth positions sounded the same when he said them. This made understanding his speech very difficult. He also did not articulate the endings of words. He just left these off completely. All of these errors had to be unlearned and then relearned correctly. This type of learning can be extremely difficult when the error has been going on for a long time. It is always easier to learn something new than to unlearn a deep rooted habit.

The reason I chose the *Sonday System I* for Michael was because of his age as well as his learning difference. The *Sonday System I* introduces each sound in the English language. Michael needed to practice making the subtle differences in each sound and to make each sound unique. This system is also research based and proven to be effective when implemented effectively. This intervention was a perfect platform for Michael's learning differences and current level, ability, and age.

Michael also began seeing a speech therapist at this time. I was able to work closely in tandem with the speech therapist to address Michael's understanding of sounds and how to make each one different. I could ask the speech therapist to work on any sounds that I needed him to pronounce more clearly at a particular time in the reading program. This helped to make the reading program very successful as well as make his speech much more understandable.

This program was also suited to Michael's age. The other two programs would be too "babyish" for him. There are many multisensory components to this program which is crucial to Michael's success in relearning and remembering the information that he learned incorrectly the first time. The *Sonday* program also uses sound cards to introduce new sounds. Words are formed with the sounds and practiced separately and then in a story format. This process uses frequent repeated practice, but using different avenues for practice, so it never seems boring or repetitious.

Since we started from the beginning, he was able to learn and practice the correct sound for each sound in the English language. I used a mirror for him to practice making some of the more difficult sounds. He would watch my mouth movements and then try to copy them while looking in the mirror. He could not feel some of these sounds so he needed to observe them closely to imitate them. The sound cards helped us to isolate each sound and then practice each sound until he was successful. Then we incorporated these sounds into words and then into stories. The *Sonday Readers* uses controlled text which matches each level of the program. This makes it easier to choose appropriate reading material for the sounds and patterns being practiced. Eventually, Michael brought books he was reading at school and these were incorporated into our reading time.

There are 36 parts or lessons to the *Sonday System I* program. Each lesson can take anywhere from one session to several sessions to complete, depending on the child's unique needs. Michael completed the *Sonday System I* in about four months.

I used a reward system to keep Michael motivated during this intervention period. He hated to read and did not want to do a reading program. I discussed the reward system with his mother. She agreed to take him shopping after he earned a certain amount of tickets. He received one ticket for each session in which he worked hard. If he did not work hard, he did not receive a ticket. After a little trial and error we settled into a system which worked for both of us.

After completing this program, his teacher commented to his mother that there was a huge change in his behavior at school. He now raised his hand all the time where before he would never volunteer to answer a question. He also entered into all of the debates in the classroom, where before he remained silent. He became much more self-confident in class and in his interactions with other children.

Mary

Mary was one month shy of seven years old. She was adopted from China and came to the U.S. at about three years old. She was found abandoned at 6 months old and almost died from tuberculosis. She was moved from hospital to orphanage to missionary home and back to orphanage for the next two years. She suffered greatly in her early years from physical pain, malnourishment, isolation and lack of stimulation and more importantly, lack of love.

Mary was speaking Chinese when she first came to the U.S but no one else spoke her dialect. She stopped speaking Chinese after about three months and just communicated using hand gestures and frequent bouts of screaming. She had major meltdowns in the beginning of her transition with her new family but the meltdowns gradually became less and less frequent and then stopped altogether. She loved to paint and draw which she did every day.

She did not speak English for another year and a half. When she did start speaking English it was only a few words, never a sentence. By five and a half she was speaking in phrases but still not complete sentences. She did not start Kindergarten until 6 to give her more time to adjust and develop. She was tested for learning differences before kindergarten but did not qualify for any services.

During Kindergarten she was given extra one on one reading services and successfully completed the year, but was still not at grade level. This is the point where I tested her and began a reading intervention program.

The testing revealed that Mary was strong in blending and segmenting skills but poor in rhyming skills. The lack of rhyming skills but strength in the other two skills seems to occur more frequently with children for which English is a second language. Blending and segmenting skills are more important at this time for reading so the lack of rhyming skills will not hold her back. She knew all the letter names and could identify 23 of the 26 beginning letter sounds. She was confusing b, d, and p letters and sounds but this was still age appropriate so not an issue yet. I included several multisensory methods to reinforce those sounds.

An informal reading inventory determined that she was at a frustrated pre-primer level which meant that she was not reading at this time. She could only identify 3 of the 20 pre-primer sight words on a list and could not identify any in a reading passage. She understood that she had to read from left to right and she knew that she must give each letter a sound to decode the words, but she was not actually using her knowledge.

She was able to sit and concentrate for stretches of time and was not easily distracted which is always beneficial to learning. Since she liked to draw, I included many exercises using a dry erase board and colored markers with art paper. My goal for this child was to take her from a non-reading level to a strong first grade reading level during our program.

I decided to use *Hooked on Phonics* for this child for several reasons. First, it was age appropriate for her as well as instructional level appropriate. The material was suited for her level and was colorful and engaging which would appeal to her artistic instincts. Second, she did not appear to have a learning difference at this time. She was behind academically, but considering her extremely difficult first three years in life, this was understandable. *Hooked on Phonics* was a good choice for a child who was behind but did not have a major learning difference.

I incorporated several additional multisensory methods into her program to help strengthen her filing and retrieving of information in her brain, especially in areas of difficulty, such as b, d, p and sight words. Some of the manipulatives I used were; a sand tray, letter cubes, letter dice, raised letter cards, sight word Bingo, air writing, dry erase board, and drawing. I put a reward system in place during our first session to help with her motivation. She chose a star for her index card after every lesson. She used her card to go "shopping" from the treasure chest. Prior to beginning the program I asked her what she liked to do and then bought items that fit her personality. She liked to do her nails, wear lip gloss, paint with watercolors and finger paint. I found items at the dollar store for all these activities and placed them in the treasure chest for different "prices" or star values.

During our first several sessions, I discovered that Mary was strongly focused for the first 20 minutes. After that, she needed to be more physically engaged in an activity to keep her interest. I used the storybook readers from the *Hooked on Phonics* program and the *Sonday* readers to incorporate our lessons into a book reading format.

She loved the dry erase board and working with the dice so we used both of these activities for word building games. The index card with stickers worked extremely well with her and was a great way to keep her motivated, especially during a difficult lesson.

I also concentrated on the Fry sight word list for her level. We began with the first 25 words in our "bank." We worked with five words at a time. When she knew the first five, we moved on to the next five words. We also wrote the words on "clouds" (colored art paper) for her to place on her walls next to her bed. This strategy exposed her to passive learning with the sight words on her wall as well as gave her the opportunity to practice reading these words before bed.

Mary completed the first level of *Hooked on Phonics* in two months working two to three times a week. She could easily decode short vowel words at the end of this period. The confusion between b, p, and d were no longer an issue for her. Sight words continued to be a problem for her to remember. Placing them on her bedroom wall made a big difference, though.

Mary continued to improve and reached grade level by the second semester of first grade. She loves to read and write her own books, with illustrations, of course.

Frank

Frank was diagnosed with Autism at the age of three. His mother researched and applied several components over the years to help him recover. Reading was one area needing extra work. His mother contacted me about suggestions for working with him at home when he was in first grade. We discussed the skills he had and where he needed to be in a mainstream age level classroom. Reading Blocks: A Step by Step Method to Teach Reading was a great fit for him. His mother and I worked closely over the phone adapting the reading program to fit Frank's unique needs and which could be implemented by her and an older sister. We communicated daily at times to monitor and adjust the program, especially in the beginning when it was new to both of them. His mother used the treasure chest motivation strategy very successfully. Their story follows and is told by Frank's mother.

"In 2003, our son was diagnosed with Autism Spectrum Disorder. At the age of three, he showed the classic symptoms of the gradual decline which began at 18 months when an otherwise normally developing child lost speech, eye contact and eventually, nearly all meaningful communication. My husband and I quickly identified the DAN protocol as the one which was achieving the greatest results so we began an intensive home ABA program, along with a gluten/casein free diet. We used some advised supplements and within six months saw enough improvement to start him in a Montessori pre-school with a helper.

Fast forward. Our son began school on time with some support from a special needs assistant. His increases were steady but, at the time, slow. Speech came last, a fact which every parent struggling with this frightening illness should know. At the age of 8 he was proceeding along at grade level, speaking well, and succeeding in every subject but reading. I knew he was having difficulty but frankly, a little trouble reading was the least of our problems, or so I thought.

That summer I asked him if he was looking forward to returning to school. He responded immediately and with a grave face, "No."

"Why not?" I asked him, alarmed.

"Because I am one of the worst readers in the class."

As every parent of a struggling reader will understand, this was like a knife wound. His self-esteem was terribly low and his confidence also terribly low. And as if communication difficulties and sensory issues were not enough, the child was terrified that he would be asked to read aloud. Denial evaporated at that moment and I said, "Would you like to be one of the best readers in the class? We can help you but you'll have to work really hard and it will have to be after school."

"I'll do anything," he responded firmly.

"Leave it with me," I said.

Thus began a research project that was as determined as our initial fact finding mission for Autism. The school, a dream team in terms of cooperating with our son's special needs, had given him extra reading help but teaching our son with the same strategies only more was not the answer. He was not improving. Additionally, his reading teacher, seeing that Frank was not benefitting from the special tutoring, wondered aloud if he would be able to handle mainstream school. If my commitment to finding the answer to Frank's reading puzzle needed any further impetus that was provided by the threat of my son being in a special needs class for the singular reason that he could not read at grade level.

After an evaluation of our son's skills and a consultation by Mrs. McCarthy we resolved that the *Reading Blocks: A Step by Step Method to Teach Reading* program had the best approach for our son's difficulties. Because there were no specialists with these strategies in on our area, we settled, once again, on a home program with the long distance assistance of Mrs. McCarthy as a consultant.

We used every suggestion she gave us and the result was that in 8 weeks our son's confidence had soared. In 12 weeks he was reading at grade level. Teaching my son to read using the multisensory strategies proposed by Mrs. McCarthy, and using the *Reading Blocks: A Step by Step Method to Teach Reading* system, was one of the most singularly gratifying experiences of my life.

Prior to this, I dreaded doing homework with my son. The idea of tackling a reading program at home seemed way out of my league. But with the given methodology, it was not only doable. It was a joy and that is the truth. The prize bag at the end of each session became the highlight of my son's day. His younger sister, determined to participate, received 15 minutes of her own reading program with the result that she went into school reading at the age of five.

My son was not a poor learner. He just needed to be taught with different senses like touch and hearing, in addition to seeing. The saddest thing to me was that he learned so fast. It was like lightening once he began to move the letters around the board to make the words. It was sad because I saw that he had struggled unnecessarily. All I can say is that over a couple of weeks, 'it clicked' and there was no stopping him then.

My advice to any parent reading this is as follows: move fast. Think for yourself. Do whatever it takes to help your child get over the block. Once they do their self-esteem sky rockets. And that is then seen in every other area. I loved that Mrs. McCarthy's approaches were all so positive and loving. The moment we explained to our son that he learned differently, and backed this up by pointing to his other strengths, like math and puzzles, he felt better about himself and cooperated fully with the program. This was a real life changer for him. For me, as a parents? I feel very grateful."

Two First Hand Accounts of Growing Up with a Learning Difference

The following two stories are written by two of the previous struggling readers. I asked each of them to tell me how it felt as a child to struggle with reading. Frank was 13 and Caitlin was 25 when this was written.

Frank

When I had trouble reading in school I felt annoyed. It was hard because I was behind in class. In the class, most people were going faster than I could go. A couple of kids were slower, but mostly they were all faster. I dreaded reading and didn't like it. It was boring because I couldn't do it. About doing the program, I remember that every day I got something from the grab bag. I really tried because I loved getting the prizes. Doing the program was not as boring as school. And I felt like I was good at the program, where in school I didn't feel like I was good at reading. Now I like reading football books, soccer books and I like reading books that do not have too much description. I loved *Diary of a Wimpy Kid*. I love reading books about defensive strategies in soccer and that teach different skills. I like writing and I keep a diary. I'm good at writing now which makes school easy. I like reading aloud in class or reading aloud anywhere. Before the program I couldn't read aloud because I couldn't really read well. The teacher didn't make me so that was good. I didn't like reading then.

My advice to a kid having trouble reading is that they should do the program because if it helped me it might help them. I probably would have had to stay back a year if I still had trouble reading but there is more to school than just reading. I would tell a kid having trouble reading to try to be good at as many things as they can, so that they can find something they can be good at, until they get better at reading. Also, kids need to listen to the teachers. If the teacher is good they'll know what they're talking about and if the teacher is bad or mean, then the kids should read their workbooks where there is advice and examples. I would also tell any other kid having trouble reading that they can get better if they try and someone helps them. They should ask for help.

Caitlin

I remember being a little girl. I remember what my teacher, the tutors, and the counselors were saying. I remember the shame and guilt because I could not do what was being asked of me. I remember how I was treated. My name is Caitlin. I may not know you or your child, but I know about the struggles they will go through in life and I know how they are feeling inside. Granted everyone is different and every parent will raise their children differently, but I can honestly tell you I would not be here like I am today if my mom had not been my advocate.

Looking back on my childhood I would say I acted like any other normal child. I was extremely energetic, outgoing and had a great imagination. I remember my first struggle in school began in preschool. I was introduced to the ABC's, counting, and tying my shoes. It felt like a dance I did not know. It felt like everyone knew the rhythm and the steps to a choreographed dance and I could not figure it out.

I proceeded to kindergarten where I was one of the select few to spend two years there, instead of one. I did not mind being held back at the time and it also allowed me to be in the same grade as my younger sister. Having a sibling in the same grade as me was a blessing in disguise all during my grammar school years. I often found myself seeking her out to explain something we were doing in class. As the years went by, I began to need more help than my sister could supply.

At this time, the Catholic school I attended did not have services for children with any kind of special learning needs. So, every day after school I would be driven over to the public school for my "lesson". I remember this clearly. The woman would empty the contents of my backpack all over the table. Books would slide everywhere, pencils fall to the ground. All she had to do was ask, I would have gotten the one textbook we needed. I remember feeling uneasy. Looking around the room I had been placed with special needs children. Something was wrong. I didn't belong there. I was scared.

I remember. I remember. I remember. I cannot stress this enough. People think because you are a child you will not remember. But we do, I did. I remember being yelled at by my teacher in front of the whole class. I remember being called stupid, many, many times. I remember how I was treated. I remember the angry disapproving faces. I remember hearing my parents talk about me, and what was wrong.

My mom was the only one who advocated for me. Of course my dad was on her side as well but it was my mom who did all the research, read the books, and talked to the doctors. It was my mom who brought me to an audiologist. Finally in the fourth grade, I was diagnosed with dyslexia and an auditory processing disorder. I remember seeing the relief in my mom's face. I remember that inspirational smile that melted my shame away. This diagnosis was all it took. My mom read every book, learned how the brain worked, and knew what was happening with me, she became the expert.

It was not easy learning how to read. I had to attend a program every day for several months. This was probably one of the hardest things I had to do in my life. I continued to struggle at times but it did not stop me from moving on.

In grammar school I was told I would be lucky to graduate high school. After I took the ACT test, I was told no college would accept me with a score like mine. I chose not to listen. Instead, I graduated from high school with honors and I was accepted into an outstanding university in the Midwest. I graduated from college, as Senior Class President, with a double major and a Bachelors of Arts degree. Now I'm finishing up my Bachelors of Science degree in Nursing.

I love to learn. I love reading books. I love knowledge. I firmly believe that knowledge is power. I am living proof of that. I still am a terrible speller but my gifts of seeing the world differently have made me successful in so many other ways. I learned how to interpret the world like everyone else does but also to add my own slant and perspective to the situation.

I would never have gotten to the point where I enjoyed reading if my mom had not fought for me to understand. I never would have understood if my mom had not fought for an answer. Looking back, I know if my mom was not my advocate I would not be the successful person I am today. Thanks mom.

If I had to give you one piece of advice from my experiences, I would tell you to fight for your child. He will be successful with your help.

Points to Ponder

- The program needs to match the child's needs.
- Every child is a unique learner. The program needs to be adjusted according to the child's needs not the other way around.
- Assessments need to occur on a regular basis.
- You must be seeing progress. If not, make a change.
- Make sure to encourage, motivate, reward, and praise regularly.
- Learning to read should be a positive experience, not a nightmare. The program is not fitting the child if the child is upset all the time. You can make adjustments to suit the child and the program.
- Be your child's strongest advocate.

Chapter 10

Detailed Description of Professional Programs

"Know what you want to do, hold the thought firmly, and do every day what should be done, and every sunset will see you that much nearer to your goal."

Elbert Hubbard

Lindamood-Bell   www.lindamoodbell.com   800-233-1819

Lindamood-Bell is a company offering programs designed by Patricia Lindamood and Nanci Bell. The programs include: *Seeing Stars; Visualizing and Verbalizing; Lindamood Phoneme Sequencing (LIPS); Talkies; and On Cloud Nine* for Mathematics. A child is first evaluated and then the director develops a learning plan incorporating the programs needed to suit the child's needs.

Seeing Stars is recommended for slow phonetic processing speed, fluency, sight words, and spelling. *Visualizing and Verbalizing* is recommended for comprehension and developing the gestalt of the passage being read. *LIPS* is recommended for phonemic awareness, reading, spelling, and connecting mouth movements to speech sounds. This gives the child more pathways in the brain for recalling specific reading information. *Talkies* is recommended for language comprehension and is a primer to the *Visualizing and Verbalizing* program for children who need this extra support. *On Cloud Nine* is a mathematics program that uses multisensory support for understanding mathematics. This is just a generalized summary of each component and you can call or go to their website for more details.

Lindamood-Bell has offices around the United States but is based in California. The company offers training seminars around the US and you can go on their website to find locations and dates. They also offer a free information seminar to introduce you to the components of their program.

Lindamood-Bell programs are delivered by instructors trained in the Lindamood-Bell methods and using their products. The instruction can occur on site in one of their program offices as well as in your home. In home instruction costs more, of course. The instruction is research based and proven effective. This program is also based on the Orton-Gillingham methods. You can call their main office to locate a center near you as well as inquire about current prices.

This program is expensive but is very successful. This is a great option if your child has severe learning differences or is far behind grade level. You can contact them to discuss your child's personal needs and to see if this program will meet your child's needs. They can evaluate your child and recommend options.

You can purchase each component of this program separately from Gander Publishing (www.ganderpublishing.com). *Seeing Stars, VV, and LIPS* cost approximately $440.00 each. They all include a large variety of materials but you do need training to effectively implement this program.

Wilson   www.wilsonlanguage.com   800-899-8454

The *Wilson* system is based on Orton-Gillingham methodology. This program is appropriate for ages seven and older, and any reading level. *Wilson* is multisensory, research based, and proven to be effective. This system follows a sequential and cumulative form of instruction. *Wilson* also uses a sound tapping system that is very effective and has a large quantity of decodable texts for reading practice.

This program is delivered by trained instructors in an office or home setting. The lessons are given three to five days a week for 60-90 minutes and can be in small groups or one-on-one. This is a 12 step process that can take anywhere from one to three years to complete, depending on person, level, and learning difference.

You can purchase the material for the program but you need training to ensure that the program is delivered according to how it was designed. There are video tapes to watch for initial training but in person seminars are required for certification as a *Wilson* trainer.

The starter kit cost $149.00 and includes steps 1-6. The standard set cost $279.00 and includes all the material for steps 1-12, or the complete program. The deluxe set cost $459.00 and includes the whole program, steps 1-12, plus video training. The sets include a substantial amount of materials for the price, including: student reader, instruction manual, rules notebook, dictation books 1-6 or 1-12, syllable cards, magnetic journal with phoneme tiles, magnetic strips, WRS student readers, word cards, sound cards, testing material, videos, and readers in the deluxe set. You can check their website for more details on specific contents.

This is a very effective program. If you want to do use this program at home with your child you will have to purchase the deluxe set for the video training. You can be effective with the video training if your child is not too far behind and does not have a severe learning difference. If your child has a severe learning issue, the program should be implemented by someone specifically trained in this program. Training in the Wilson program is crucial for the highest level of success.

Points to Ponder

Lindamood-Bell and Wilson programs are both:

- Research based
- Explicit, Systematic, Multisensory, and Cumulative Instruction
- Based on Orton-Gillingham methods
- Systematic and cumulative instruction
- Products are available for purchase
- Need training to implement
- Office clinic setting as well as in-home setting
- Similar in price
- Offer workshop training
- Lindamood-Bell's intense program can move a child up several grades in a few months. (Every situation is unique.)
- Wilson offers video training
- Wilson might have a trainer trying to accumulate hours for certification and could offer discounted price.
- Not a great choice for at-home instruction by parent unless you receive intensive training.
- These two programs are better implemented by professionally trained instructors.
- Both programs are very effective.

Chapter 11

Detailed Description of At-Home Programs

"Surround yourself with the dreamers and the doers, the believers and thinkers, but most of all , surround yourself with those who see the greatness within you, even when you don't see it yourself."

Edmund Lee

Reading Blocks: A Step by Step Method to Teach Reading

The whole program is contained in one book. The cost of the book is 39.95. Several inexpensive office supplies complete the program (binder, file folders, post it notes, marker, dry erase board). Activity pages are intentionally left blank on the back side so they can be torn out of the book and cut up to be used for each of the block's activities. Mini books are also included for each block and can be torn out, put together and stapled for reading and rereading. The activities for each block can be kept in a ziplock bag and reused to practice any component of the reading process as needed.

The introduction discusses the following: What does a learning disability or learning difference look like; the process of learning to read; seven components in learning to read; the most effective way to teach reading; explains the Reading Blocks method; explains how to use the Reading Blocks method; multisensory methods and techniques; and reward system.

Section I contains information on how to build a reader's "Reading Wall" and includes the Reading Wall assessment and instructions on how to implement this assessment prior to beginning the instruction. Dr. Fry's 1000 sight words are also included in this section. The Fry Sight Words are the top 1000 words in print. Dr. Fry listed them in the order of frequency of occurring in print. They are also included in each of the 32 reading blocks but are sorted by their phonetic properties rather than their frequency of occurring in print. Sight words should be memorized which will help to increase the reader's fluency.

This section also includes instructions for preparing a Plan of Action, preparing the file folder and binder which will be used in the instruction. There is also a detailed explanation of a learning strategy to be used after each block, motivation techniques, and instructions and recommendations for the first instructional session.

Section II contains the 32 reading blocks. Each reading block contains the information that needs to be learned as well as activities to practice the material in a multisensory manner. The multisensory activities will help the reader to file and retrieve the information from the brain. Each block should be learned in its entirety before moving on to the next block. There is a checkpoint after every five blocks to check if the material is understood correctly and remembered. The last checkpoint covers the last seven blocks. The checkpoints can also be used in the beginning of the program to help determine if any of the blocks can be skipped.

I always keep a notebook for each person I tutor. I jot down notes of things I observed during the lesson such as areas of strengths or weaknesses. Post-it notes are also a quick way to take a note to remind you about re-teaching a particular skill or an area that needs more practice. The post-it notes can be kept in the file folder and will remind you to include in the next lesson. You want to keep track of skills that are fun for the child as well as skills that are difficult for the child and could use more practice. You can always incorporate more practice for something that was difficult into the next lesson. You can also repeat any lesson until your child has mastered the material.

Video lessons are also available for download. Each video corresponds to a reading block. The videos can be used to teach the lesson or to review a lesson. The videos can be purchased separately or as a complete program.

I would also recommend using the series of decodable books called "*The Sonday System Readers.*" for more reading practice. These books are not mandatory but make a great addition to your reading program. This series can be found at www.winsorlearning.com and costs approximately $75.00 for a set of 15 decodable readers.

Another good set of books to use with any reading instruction program is called *The Alphabet Series* and can be viewed on my website: www.TheReadingTutor.org . *The Alphabet Series* starter set costs approximately $134.00 and consists of 39 decodable texts which are great for reading levels kindergarten through third grade. These readers are also not mandatory but a great addition to any reading session.

Both sets offer decodable text which is like a having a set of training wheels for a new or struggling reader. Each book in both series is a little more advanced than the previous title which offers more reading support and practice while increasing reading skills. Reading Blocks recommends which story to use that will match the skill level of the block. Reading Blocks includes one mini story in each block that contains skills learned in that block as well as previous blocks but these books offer additional supported reading practice. I recommend ending every session with a 10 – 30 minute book reading session depending on the reader's age and how quickly the day's lesson was completed.

The book reading time at the end of a session connects the isolated skill practice to the real goal of reading, which is some form of message exchange between the writer and the reader. You can also send a book home for the individual to practice, by himself or to read to his family members. I always tell the individual to read the book to his dog, his fish, his stuffed animals, his parents, his spouse if that is the case, his siblings, and/or anyone else that will sit still long enough to listen which will enable him to practice his newly learned skills.

The *Reading Blocks: A Step by Step Method to Teach Reading* system and videos is effective and inexpensive and will be a good fit for the majority of learners.

Sonday System I

The Sonday System I is appropriate for reading levels grade one and grade two and age levels six and above. The cost of this program is currently $449.00. You can find this program at: www.winsorlearning.com.

You can use this program with an older child who is reading at a first grade level because it is not "babyish". I recommend this program for several reasons. First, it is very easy to use which is important for a person without a teaching or reading background. I love the way the program is organized and executed. All the materials you need to complete the program are included so you don't have to make or buy anything else. The only items I would add to this program are the decodable readers which I mentioned above.

You also do not need any outside specialized training in the execution of this system. The training you do need is included on a DVD as well as a CD of sound pronunciations. The DVD is a great training tool and helps a novice reading instructor to tutor in a way that will ensure success.

The pronunciation CD is good for showing the tutor the correct way to pronounce the sounds. Many people add an "uh" sound after the letter sound which confuses the child. For example, the letter d should be pronounced /d/ and not /duh/. The sound is clipped short but we try to emphasize the sound by adding the /uh/. The /duh/ sound is really two letters, d and u.

This program consists of: A Learning Plan book with five pre-reading lessons and 36 reading lessons, the instructional DVD, word book, 25 reading strips, sound cards, blend cards, 11 packs of word card decks, music CD, board game and pieces, 52 printing practice pages, upper and lower case alphabet strips, 52 letter tactile cards, audio pronunciation CD, pre and post tests and mastery checks for reading.

There are a total of 36 reading lessons and five pre-reading lessons. I would recommend beginning with the first lesson even if your child knows some of this material. If the material is already mastered by your child you can complete the lesson quickly and it will be a good review. It will also help your child to feel confident that he can be successful with this program. Starting at the beginning will ensure that you fill in any missing gaps that your child may have and you don't want to leave out any material.

You should be able to complete one lesson during each 40 minute session. I like to end each session with reading a book which the child can also reread at bedtime or any other time during the day.

The letter tactile cards are a great multisensory tool for teaching the letters and sounds. The cards have a raised edge and arrows to follow when tracing with a finger. I have also made tactile alphabet cards using glue sprinkled with sand before it dries so there is a rough raised bubble over the letter. This helps the child who is having difficulty remembering letter names and sounds. The child can say the sound while tracing the letter card.

Sonday System I begins with five pre-reading levels. This section covers alphabet knowledge and phonemic awareness skills. For example, can your child point to each letter in any random order and give the name and sound of the letter? Can your child tell you the beginning, middle or end sound for any three sound word (cat)? These are pre-reading skills. When these skills are mastered, the child can begin level one.

There are 36 reading levels. Each follows the same format but covers different reading knowledge which increases in difficulty as you advance through the levels. The format includes: Read Sounds, Spell Sounds, Introduce New Sounds, Review New Sound, and Read Aloud. Each section gives you the letters, sounds, and words to practice. The section also tells you where to find more material to use for more practice.

A pad of paper is included which is configured to match what you are doing in each lesson. I glue one of these papers on each of eight different colored construction papers, and then laminate them. This makes them usable with dry erase markers and they can be reused over and over. This also gives the child a choice of their favorite color to use. I also let them choose their favorite color marker to use for each lesson. It is just a little choice but kids always love to make this choice. I think it gives children a little control over their lesson which helps to make them more involved in the lesson.

Another component I add to the beginning lessons is to have letter tiles to use for saying sounds and making words. I like to practice with something concrete that the child can touch and move about and then do the writing. I also keep a sand tray handy for additional practice with any difficult sounds or reversal of letters such as b and d. The tiles can be found in a teacher store and sometimes in a dollar store. You can make a sand tray with a baking sheet or tray and any kind of sand. Paint the bottom of the tray or use a colored surface on the bottom so you will have a strong contrast between the bottom color and the sand. This makes the letter stand out more that the child traces into the sand. Always have the child repeat the sound of the letter as he traces the letter in the sand.

After every three levels, there is a Mastery Check. This is the assessment component. The child reads a set of 20 words and then writes a set of 20 words. The results of this check help you to determine if your child has mastered this level and can move on to the next. If your child has not mastered the material, you will create a learning plan using the form provided in your materials.

The learning plan will cover any material you need to practice more and the material you intend to use for the practice. For example, if after completing levels one to three, your child reads "sat" as "sap" and "mat" as "map" you would write down the letter "t" on your learning plan. Then you would look in the word book for the page that has words to practice the letter t and you would write down this page number. Then you would decide how you wanted to practice this letter. One way, for example, would be to write the letter in the sand tray at the beginning of several sessions. You would also include this in your learning plan. When you begin your next session, you look at your learning plan for what to include in this session. This is just a simplified example. Your learning plan will be more involved, especially as you advance to more difficult material.

All the directions and materials are included so you just have to follow along with the program. You do not have to develop anything on your own. After repeating the material, you give the mastery check again. You can move to the next level when each check is mastered. The mastery checks help you to ensure that the child has really mastered the material before moving forward and adding more new material. This adds to the success level of the program.

As you advance, sight words are introduced and practiced in each session. Sight words cannot always be sounded out and need to be memorized. These are words that are seen very frequently in every book so it is important to memorize these words as they come up. You can make a sight word bank or file box. I always have two piles for sight words. One pile is made up of all the words the child can read easily and the other pile is more difficult words. When the child has read the word correctly and quickly for three consecutive sessions, the word is moved to the easy pile. You can use these words for sight word Bingo or memory games or various card games such as Go Fish.

I would also recommend putting them around your house and your child's bedroom walls. The refrigerator is also a good place for the magnetic letters. Everyone is frequently in the kitchen so this is an ideal place for extra practice that no one really notices. The child will practice reading them without even knowing it if they are placed all around his environment. Remember, this is only temporary. You won't have words all over your house forever.

You continue on with all the lessons until the end. When your child has successfully completed and mastered each of the 36 levels he will be at the end of second grade /beginning of third grade reading level. If your child is older and needs to be at a higher level, or if you just want to continue to give your child a reading advantage, you can continue on with the *Sonday System II*.

The *Sonday System II* follows the same format as *Sonday System I* but at a higher reading level. This program starts off with an assessment which checks for mastery of skills in *System I* and then begins where *System I* left off. *Sonday System I and II* are a complete reading program which cover reading material to approximately an eighth grade reading level.

Hooked On Phonics

The *Hooked on Phonics* complete set includes five sets of materials. Each set builds on the previous set and all five sets cover reading material to approximately the third grade reading level. Each set consists of a workbook covering the skills being taught at this level, small storybooks to practice skills at this level in a narrative format, sound flash cards and matching cassette with the sounds recorded for additional practice, a poster and stickers for incentive, and sight word cards for the level. Level one also has a CD or cassette tape of sound pronunciations to follow along using the alphabet cards, a CD or cassette with phonics songs, and a CD for computer practice for skills learned in level one. There is also a parents' guide for additional information and suggestions for completing each level in the program.

Each level in this program follows the same format. The child can listen to a cassette of sounds for the level and follow with the sound cards provided. You can also show the child the card and have him just tell you the sound. Use whatever way works best for the child.

Next he reads from the workbook. The workbook builds words using the sounds being practiced. There is a lot of repetition and practice for each sound or set of sounds. The workbook also has word building practice using alphabet cards and spots to stop and read a storybook. The storybook incorporates words and sounds previously covered. This format breaks up the monotony of just reading words, as well as ties the separate reading skills into actual book reading which is the ultimate goal.

I believe this program is effective and fun to use for five to eight year olds. You can use this program with an older child who is reading at this level, but you need to be sensitive as to how the child feels using this material. Some children will be ok with younger material and others will be extremely embarrassed.

Hooked on Phonics is easy to follow. You can work 20 -30 minutes with a younger child and up to 45 minutes with an older child. I would not work more than 45 minutes during a session because the child will be tired and will not retain the information as well.

The child can always read silently for some additional reading practice. For example, if the child is six years old, you might want to work together for 20 minutes if it is somewhat difficult, or 30 minutes if the child is still actively engaged. Then spend 10 – 20 minutes reading a storybook from this level. They can also re-read any storybook that is easy for them at any time during the program. Re-reading an easy book is great practice for building their fluency (reading speed).

The time spent on each session will depend on the material being covered, the disposition of the child at this moment in time, and the disposition of the teacher. You will find that sometimes you are both working great and you want to keep going at those times. Other times one or both of you are having a difficult day and it is best to not press too hard or work too long during those times. Older children can usually work longer than the younger ones but again it all depends on the individual. You should fall into a system after a few sessions when you both learn how to work together.

You can add some multisensory materials to this set very inexpensively which will increase the program's effectiveness. I like to use a sand tray, dry erase board and markers, letter cubes or tiles, and raised alphabet cards. I use these extras mainly with the first level and sometimes higher levels to reinforce a skill that continues to be difficult for the child. The sand tray is great for reinforcing difficult sounds like /b/ /p/ and /d/ as well as sight word practice. I like to use the dry erase boards for word building practice and the dice and cubes for word building games. You can easily make a BINGO letter sound game or sight word game using the materials provided and some of the extras.

The *Sonday Readers* are also a very useful addition to this set for additional practice using controlled text. The readers that come with each level are perfect for the necessary narrative practice with each new skill being taught. The readers are colorful and engaging and a very effective form of practice for the newly budding reading skills.

As with all the other programs, some form of motivational system inspires the child to work even harder. Tickets and prizes are always fun but use whatever works with your child and your situation.

Points to Ponder

- *Reading Blocks: A Step by Step Method to Teach Reading* is an appropriate choice for: anyone teaching reading, especially with individuals with learning differences (disabilities); recommended for all age levels; very inexpensive; is very effective; is a researched based method; is a multisensory based method; is easy to implement; offers systematic instruction; is extremely thorough in presenting reading material; has a corresponding video teaching component that matches each lesson for additional support.

- *Sonday System I* is an appropriate choice for: Reading levels kindergarten to third grade and age levels from 5-13; effective; systematic instruction; extremely thorough in presenting reading material; research based; multisensory instruction.

- *Sonday System II* is an appropriate choice for: Reading levels third grade to eighth grade and age levels 7-15 (approximately); effective, systematic instruction; extremely thorough in presenting reading material; research based; multisensory instruction.

- *Hooked on Phonics* is an appropriate choice for: Reading levels kindergarten to early third grade and age levels of five to eight (approximately); effective and easy to implement; systematic instruction; thorough in presenting reading material; includes leveled readers; somewhat multisensory; is research based.

Chapter 12

Multisensory Activities for Teaching Reading

"The line between failure and success is so fine that we scarcely know when we pass it; so fine that we are often on the line and do not know it. "

Elbert Hubbard

An activity can be considered multisensory when more than one sense is used to complete a task. For example, tracing a letter on sandpaper while saying the sound aloud is a multisensory activity. This double action simultaneously activates more than one pathway in the neural systems of the brain, which helps the child to remember the targeted task.

You want to build a strong pathway in the brain for the necessary phonological information for reading. This is done with explicit instruction and repeated practice. Picture the brain like an open field. You travel through that field every day for a shortcut. Eventually, there is a pathway worn into the grass from taking that shortcut. We want to develop these pathways in the brain which are necessary for reading effectively. Good readers already have these pathways but struggling readers can develop these pathways with the appropriate instruction and repeated practice.

The following are several methods which can be used when a child is struggling to remember the sounds of the alphabet. They can also be used for practicing how to blend and segment sounds, and when learning new sight words.

- Pour a layer of sand on a tray or cookie sheet. The sand should be a contrasting color to the bottom of the tray. For example, if the bottom of the tray is blue, the sand can be yellow. You can paint the bottom of the tray. The sand can be bought in a color or dyed. The child writes the targeted letter while saying the sound aloud. The child sees the color contrast between the bottom of the tray and the color of the sand, feels the coarseness of the sand against his finger while he outlines the letter, and hears his voice making the sound as well as feels the movements in the mouth making the sound. The child can use this for writing and saying sight words

- First, show a letter and say the sound. Then have the child air write the letter using the whole arm, not just the wrist, while saying the sound. The child's eyes should be closed and the child is instructed to visualize the letter she is making on a particular colored board and a particular color letter. For example, he can visualize himself writing a red letter on a black chalkboard. Now you have large muscle movement, hearing the sound, and visualizing the colored letter.

- Write each letter on a colored square of tag board or cardboard. Copy over the letter with a bubble layer of glue and sprinkle sand over the glue. When this is dry, you can use the letters for tracing over while saying the sound. The child feels the texture, sees the color, and hears the sound. You can also buy fat plastic letters that have a bumpy texture on the top. These are great for feeling the formation of letter, while at the same time, saying the sound of the letter.

- Have the child use his finger to write the letter on his thigh or upper arm while saying the sound. The child has muscle movement of writing the letter, hears the sound, and feels the letter being formed on his thigh or upper arm. I also used my finger to trace the letter on my daughter's back and she had to guess the letter and then say the sound. The child feels the formation of the letter and has to visualize the letter and then retrieve the name and sound. This is more difficult and should be used on letters already practiced.
- Make letters out of clay. Then make words out of clay. Form the letter and then trace and say the sound.
- The child can use a stick or pencil to tap each sound she hears in a word. This helps the child to segment the word into sounds and to realize that each sound has its own tap.
- Have the child use her fingers to count out each sound in a word. Each sound gets one finger. This is very helpful when sounding out unknown words later on. We "count" the sounds aloud.
- Have the child take one large step for every sound in a word. "March" out the sounds. For example, "cat" would be /c/ /a/ /t/ so three large steps.
- Use colored blocks to break a word into sounds. One color for each sound heard. Have the child move each block towards him for each sound in the word. When all the sounds are brought down and sounded he then reads the word. You can also use colored tag board or cardboard with one square drawn on the top third of the paper, two squares drawn together in the middle third of the paper, and three squares drawn together on the bottom third of the paper. The word cat would be formed by putting a different colored block into each of the three squares which are on the bottom third of the paper. This uses muscle movement, visual activation, and sound. The squares also give the child a visual tangible way to see the three sounds in the one word. This helps the child to understand that the sounds in the word are separate, and he can "see" how he can say each one separately.
- You can purchase dice that have alphabet letters on them instead of numbers. You can play a game of making words by throwing the alphabet dice and trying to make words from the letters which land up. Use the squares again to form one, two, and three letter words. You can also play this game with sounds. He can throw the dice and then get one point for every sound he can identify on the dice. He can write the letters thrown on a dry erase board and say each sound as he writes it.
- Use letter tiles to form words. Again, use the square boxes. Place one tile into one box. The letter tiles are also great for making and changing words. For example, start with four consonant letter tiles and one vowel letter tile, (p,t,s,c,a.) Make "cat" with the tiles. Child pulls each letter down and places in a box. Then ask the child to change "cat" to "pat". Child has to decide which sound is different, move the changed letter up, and move the new letter down. Then ask him to count the three new sounds in the word using his fingers or tapping a pencil.
- Use a dry erase board or chalkboard to write letters and words. Use different colored markers. Always have the child read the word after he has written it, or say the sound if he is at that level.

- Make little paper books out of the sounds he knows first. Then make books out of the words he knows. Then make books out of the sentences he can read. Finally make books out of stories that he makes up using all the words he has practiced. These can be used for practicing his skills. When the child is having a difficult time remembering the sounds of the letters, make an alphabet book together, one sound at a time, and use the glue and colorful sand technique. For example, start with the sound "m". Have the child write the letter on an index card or square of paper. Then have the child trace over the letter with white glue and sprinkle with colored sand. Let this dry and then have the child trace over this letter and say the sound. When he can remember this sound easily, add another sound and repeat the process. When you get to five consonant sounds add the short vowel sound of "a". Now you can also practice blending and segmenting two and three sound words. You can punch a hole into the squares or index cards and clip with a metal ring. Now he has a little book of sounds and/or words that he can read and practice.
- When practicing reading these little books, have the child read the sounds or words into a telephone. You can buy a plastic telephone handset at a teacher supply store. The child speaks into the one end and hears the sound or word from the other end. This is a great multisensory way to practice and remember the sounds and words.
- Use colorful magnetic letter tiles on the refrigerator. Start with practicing sounds and then with making words. Families spend a large portion of their time in the kitchen so it is a great place to keep some type of letter and word practice station. You can say the word of an ingredient in the dinner you are making and the child can find the corresponding letter magnet, or even write the word. You can be creative here in how you practice what needs to be practiced.
- Write the letters you are practicing on colored cardboard and place on the wall around the child's bed. Use a pointer stick to practice reading the letters and sounds before bed. You can begin with a few letters and add more as he learns the first ones. You can move on to sight words after he knows all the letter names and sounds of the letters. You can play quick little five minute games with these letters. For example, "I am thinking of a letter that makes the /a/ sound, and he says the letter name "ae". You can switch up the order with you saying the sound and him pointing to the letter that makes that sound. You can also play games with reading the sight words when they are up there. For example, "I am thinking of a word that starts with the /a/ sound." Then the child reads all the words on the wall that start with the /a/ sound until he guesses the correct word. He will not even realize that he his practicing his reading when it is in a game format. Make sure to make this fun. Do not put a whole bunch of words he cannot read on the wall around him and expect him to want to play this "game" before bed. He is tired for one, and does not want to spend more time doing something he cannot do. Practice the word first so he is familiar with it, and when he can usually get the word correct, then put it on the wall. Keep adding more sight words as he becomes fluent with the ones up there.
- Always have tons of books to read at many different reading levels and interest levels by his bed. I like to have a basket for each child next to their bed that has books they are currently reading or interested in reading soon. Having a basket of six or seven books

that are at the child's reading level or interest level makes the books more accessible than having 300 books in a book case. That becomes too overwhelming for some children.

- Also have pens, markers, crayons, journals, dry erase boards, and paper for writing and reading activities, easily accessible. I keep a whole cabinet in my kitchen just for writing and drawing materials. Replace the items as needed. Also keep writing materials in the child's bedroom. Encourage the child to write as well as to read. They are inverse operations and will each reinforce the other. The child can write his own stories or plans that he want to make. Do not worry about spelling when the child is writing in his journal. Encourage him to sound out the word he wants to spell. Spell it for him if he asks you of course, but spelling is not important in this situation. What is important is that he can take a word, and then a whole thought, from his brain, and attach sounds and letters to that word and later the whole thought. Spelling is important but just not when a person is getting their thoughts on paper. A final copy of an assignment should be spelled correctly, but a journal is for being creative and organizing thoughts.
- Some children benefit by using the Irlen colored overlays. These are plastic overlays that can be placed over the page of a book. There are several different colors and usually a child prefers one color over the others. Some children experience greater success with reading when using these overlays and it is definitely worth mentioning.
- I always try to incorporate a variety of color into the reading lesson. Color provides for choices for the child which gives the child an opportunity to experience some control over the lesson. Color also stimulates areas in the brain and the more good stimulation, the better.

There are a multitude of methods for making any lesson more multisensory. *Word Play, Brain Gym,* and *Learning to Read is Child's Play,* are three books that have great multisensory activities for struggling readers.

Conclusion

Research has shown that a good reader activates different areas of his brain than a struggling reader. These pathways seem to work automatically in a good reader. This child will seem to learn to read almost effortlessly while a struggling reader works so hard and just cannot seem to "get it."

Research has also shown that a struggling reader can be taught to use the same areas of the brain that a good reader uses. A child with a reading difficulty can develop new pathways in his brain which will enable him to read fluently. This takes repeated practice using explicit techniques but is very "doable." This is easier to accomplish with a younger child and the earlier the difficulty is discovered the better. An older child can become a fluent reader as well but there are usually difficult and faulty habits and patterns to undo and relearn. This takes more time but can definitely by accomplished.

There are many very effective programs to help a struggling reader develop reading fluency. The program you choose needs to be systematic, explicit, and cumulative. In other words, the program should teach in small "chunks" of information, in a definite order which builds upon each previous lesson. The lesson should be taught using multisensory techniques, active movements, tangible objects, and require active participation of the child. The program might be difficult but it should also be fun. Practice should be included using real books and not just isolated drills and worksheets. All of the programs discussed here teach reading in this manner.

Use this book as a jumping off point. Continue with more research directly related to your child's unique needs or learning style. If something you try fails, try something else. Your child can and will be successful in reading with your help, encouragement, and patience.

You may have noticed the message in all of the quotes introducing each new chapter. Success first begins in the mind. Help your child to view his learning difference as an asset. Escort him to the point of **knowing** that he will be successful **because** of his learning difference, not **in spite of** his learning difference. Great gifts accompany this style of learning and he will discover his gifts when he has confidence in himself and his abilities. The more confidence you can instill in your child, the more effort he will put forth to overcome this challenge. First and foremost, he must think he can. Otherwise, he won't.

My Wage

I bargained with Life for a penny,
And Life would pay no more,
However I begged at evening
When I counted my scanty store;

For Life is a just employer,
He gives you what you ask,
But once you have set the wages,
Why, you must bear the task.

I worked for a menial's hire,
only to learn, dismayed,
that any wage I had asked of Life,
Life would have gladly paid!

J.B. Rittenhouse

Appendix

Recommended Reading

Brain Gym, Teacher's Edition Revised; Paul E. Dennison, Ph.D., Gail E. Dennison

Word Play: *Fun Games for Building Reading and Writing Skills in Children with Learning Differences*; Lori Goodman and Lora Myers

Learning to Read is Child's Play; Mary Ellen Maunz, Celeste A. Matthews, Ph.D., Randall C. Klein

Recipe for Reading: Intervention Strategies for Struggling Readers; Francis Bloom and Nina Traub

Overcoming Dyslexia; A New and Complete Science-Based Program for Reading Problems at Any Level, Sally Shaywitz MD

How to Teach Reading; For Teachers, Parents and Tutors, Edward Fry, Ph.D.

Building the Reading Brain: Prek-3; Patricia Wolfe and Pamela Nevills

How the Special Needs Brain Learns; David Sousa

Smart But Scattered: The Revolutionary "Executive Skills" Approach to Helping Kids Reach Their Potential; Peg Dawson, Ed.D, and Richard Guare, Ph.D.

The Great Memory Book; Karen Markowitz, MA, Eric Jenson

Brain Compatible Strategies: Hundreds of Easy to Use Brain-Compatible Activities that Boost Attention, Motivation, Learning, and Achievement; Eric Jenson

When the Brain Can't Hear: Unraveling the Mystery of Auditory Processing Disorder; Teri James Bellis, Ph.D.

Different Brains, Different Learners: How to Reach the Hard to Reach; Eric Jenson

Words Their Way Series; www.pearsonhighered.com

Leveled Readers

Please visit my website for more information on the following leveled readers and more:
www.TheReadingTutor.org .

The Sonday System Readers

Word Family Readers

The Alphabet Series

Go Phonics

Dr. Maggie's Phonics Readers

Little Angel Readers

25 Read and Write Mini-Books That Teach Word Families, by Nancy Sanders and Anne Kennedy

Dr. Fry's 1000 Sight Words

1. the	21. at	41. there	61. some	81. my
2. of	22. be	42. use	62. her	82. than
3. and	23. this	43. an	63. would	83. first
4. a	24. have	44. each	64. make	84. water
5. to	25. from	45. which	65. like	85. been
6. in	26. or	46. she	66. him	86 called
7. is	27. one	47. do	67. into	87. who
8. you	28. had	48. how	68. time	88. am
9. that	29. by	49. their	69. has	89. its
10. it	30. words	50. if	70. look	90. now
11. he	31. but	51. will	71. two	91. find
12. was	32. not	52. up	72. more	92. long
13. for	33. what	53. other	73. write	93. down
14. on	34. all	54. about	74. go	94. day
15. are	35. were	55. out	75. see	95. did
16. as	36. we	56. many	76. number	96. get
17. with	37. when	57. then	77. no	97. come
18. his	38. your	58. them	78. way	98. made
19. they	39. can	59. these	79. could	99. May
20. I	40. said	60. so	80. people	100. part

101. over	121. name	141. boy	161. such	181. change
102. new	122. good	142. following	162. because	182. off
103. sound	123. sentence	143. came	163. turn	183. play
104. take	124. man	144. want	164. here	184. spell
105. only	125. think	145. show	165. why	185. air
106. little	126. say	146. also	166. asked	186. away
107. work	127. great	147. around	167. went	187. animals
108. know	128. where	148. farm	168. men	188. house
109. place	129. help	149. three	169. read	189. point
110. years	130. through	150. small	170. need	190. page
111. live	131. much	151. set	171. land	191. letters
112. me	132. before	152. put	172. different	192. mother
113. back	133. line	153. end	173. home	193. answer
114. give	134. right	154. does	174. us	194. found
115. most	135. too	155. another	175. move	195. study
116. very	136. means	156. well	176. try	196. still
117. after	137. old	157. large	177. kind	197. learn
118. thing	138. any	158. must	178. hand	198. should
119. our	139. same	159. big	179. picture	199. America
120. just	140. tell	160. even	180. again	200. world

201. high	221. light	241. life	261. sea	281. Watch
202. every	222. thought	242. always	262. began	282. Far
203. near	223. head	243. those	263. grow	283. indians
204. add	224. under	244. both	264. took	284. really
205. food	225. story	245. paper	265. river	285. almost
206. between	226. saw	246. together	266. four	286. let
207. own	227. left	247. got	267. carry	287. above
208. below	228. don't	248. group	268. state	288. girl
209. country	229. few	249. often	269. once	289 sometimes
210. plants	230. while	250. run	270. book	290 mountains
211. last	231. along	251. important	271. hear	291. cut
212. school	232. might	252. until	272. stop	292. young
213. father	233. close	253. children	273. without	293. talk
214. keep	234. something	254. side	274. second	294. soon
215. trees	235. seemed	255. feet	275. later	295. list
216. never	236. next	256. car	276. miss	296. song
217. started	237. hard	257. miles	277. idea	297. being
218. city	238. open	258. night	278. enough	298. leave
219. earth	239. example	259. walked	279. eat	299. family
220. eyes	240. beginning	260. white	280. face	300. it's

301. body	321. usually	341. hours	361. five	381. cold
302. music	322. didn't	342. black	362. step	382. cried
303. color	323. friends	343. products	363. morning	383. plan
304. stand	324. easy	344. happened	364. passed	384. notice
305. sun	325. heard	345. whole	365. vowel	385. south
306. questions	326. order	346. measure	366. true	386. sing
307. fish	327. red	347. remember	367. hundred	387. war
308. area	328. door	348. early	368. against	388. ground
309. mark	329. sure	349. waves	369. pattern	389. fall
310. dog	330. become	350. reached	370. numeral	390. king
311. horse	331. top	351. listen	371. table	391. town
312. birds	332. ship	352. wind	372. north	392. I'll
313. problem	333. across	353. rock	373. slowly	393. unit
314. complete	334. today	354. space	374. money	394. figure
315. room	335. during	355. covered	375. map	395. certain
316. knew	336. short	356. fast	376. busy	396. field
317. since	337. better	357. several	377. pulled	397. travel
318. ever	338. best	358. hold	378. draw	398. wood
319. piece	339. however	359. himself	379. voice	399. fire
320. told	340. low	360. toward	380. seen	400. upon

401. done	421. front	441. stay	461. warm	481. object
402. English	422. feel	442. green	462. common	482. bread
403. road	423. fact	443. known	463. bring	483. rule
404. halt	424. inches	444. island	464. explain	484. among
405. ten	425. street	445. week	465. dry	485. noun
406. fly	426. decided	446. less	466. though	486. power
407. gave	427. contain	447. machine	467. language	487. cannot
408. box	428. course	448. base	468. shape	488. able
409. finally	429. surface	449. ago	469. deep	489. six
410. wait	430. produce	450. stood	470. thousands	490. size
411. correct	431. building	451. plane	471. yes	491. dark
412. oh	432. ocean	452. system	472. clear	492. ball
413. quickly	433. class	453. behind	473. equation	493. material
414. person	434. note	454. ran	474. yet	494. special
415. became	435. nothing	455. round	475. government	495. heavy
416. shown	436. rest	456. boat	476. filled	496. fine
417. minutes	437. carefully	457. game	477. heat	497. pair
418. strong	438. scientists	458. force	478. full	498. circle
419. verb	439. inside	459. brought	479. hot	499. include
420. stars	440. wheels	460. understand	480. check	500. Built

501. can't	521. region	541. window	561. arms	581. west
502. matter	522. Return	542 difference	562. brother	582. lay
503. square	523. believe	543. distant	563. race	583. weather
504. syllables	524. dance	544. heart	564. present	584. root
505. perhaps	525. members	545. sit	565. beautiful	585instruments
506. bill	526. picked	546. sum	566. store	586. meet
507. felt	527. simple	547. summer	567. job	587. third
508. suddenly	528. cells	548. wall	568. edge	588. months
509. test	529. paint	549. forest	569. past	589. paragraph
510. direction	530. mind	550. probably	570. sign	590. raised
511. center	531. love	551. legs	571. record	591. represent
512. farmers	532. cause	552. sat	572. finished	592. soft
513. ready	533. rain	553. main	573. discovered	593. whether
514. anything	534. exercise	554. winter	574. wild	594. clothes
515. divided	535. eggs	555. wide	575. happy	595. flowers
516. general	536. train	556. written	576. beside	596. shall
517. energy	537. blue	557. length	577. gone	597. teacher
518. subject	538. wish	558. reason	578. sky	598. held
519. Europe	539. drop	559. kept	579. glass	599. describe
520. moon	540. developed	560. interest	580. million	600. Drive

601. cross	621. buy	641. temperature	661. possible	681. fraction
602. speak	622. century	642. bright	662. gold	682. Africa
603. solve	623. outside	643. lead	663. milk	683. killed
604. appear	624. everything	644. everyone	664. quiet	684. melody
605. metal	625. tall	645. method	665. natural	685. bottom
606. son	626. already	646. section	666. lot	686. trip
607. either	627. instead	647. lake	667. stone	687. hole
608. ice	628. phrase	648. consonant	668. act	688. poor
609. sleep	629. soil	649. within	669. build	689. let's
610. village	630. bed	650. dictionary	670. middle	690. fight
611. factors	631. copy	651. hair	671. speed	691. surprise
612. result	632. free	652. age	672. count	692. French
613. jumped	633. hope	653. amount	673. cat	693. died
614. snow	634. spring	654. scale	674. someone	694. beat
615. ride	635. case	655. pounds	675. sail	695. exactly
616. care	636. laughed	656. although	676. rolled	696. remain
617. floor	637. nation	657. per	677. bear	697. dress
618. hill	638. quite	658. broken	678. wonder	698. iron
619. pushed	639. type	659. moment	679. smiled	699. couldn't
620. baby	640. themselves	660. tiny	680. angle	700. Fingers

701. row	721. grew	741. east	761. suppose	781. direct
702. least	722. skin	742. pay	762. woman	782. ring
703. catch	723. valley	743. single	763. coast	783. serve
704. climbed	724. cents	744. touch	764. bank	784. child
705. wrote	725. key	745. information	765. period	785. desert
706. shouted	726. president	746. express	766. wire	786. increase
707. continued	727. brown	747. mouth	767. choose	787. history
708. itself	728. trouble	748. yard	768. clean	788. cost
709. else	729. cool	749. equal	769 visit	789. maybe
710. plains	730. cloud	750. decimal	770. bit	790. business
711. gas	732. lost	751. yourself	771. whose	791. separate
712. England	732. sent	752. control	772. received	792. break
713. burning	733. symbols	753. practice	773. garden	793. Uncle
714. design	734. wear	754. report	774. please	794. hunting
715. joined	735. bad	755. straight	775. strange	795. flow
716. foot	736. save	756. rise	776. caught	796. lady
717. law	737. experiment	757. statement	777. fell	797. students
718. ears	738. engine	758. stick	778. team	798. human
719. grass	739. alone	759. party	779. God	799. art
720. you're	740. drawing	760. seeds	780. captain	800. feeling

801. supply	821. fit	841. sense	861. position	881. meat
802. corner	822. addition	842. string	862. entered	882. lifted
803. electric	823. belong	843. blow	863. fruit	883. process
804. insects	824. safe	844. famous	864. tied	884. army
805. crops	825. soldiers	845. value	865. rich	885. hat
806. tone	826. guess	846. wings	866. dollars	886. property
807. hit	827. silent	847. movement	867. send	887. particular
808. sand	828. trade	848. pole	868. sight	888. swim
809. doctor	829. rather	849. exciting	869. chief	889. terms
810. provide	830. compare	850. branches	870. Japanese	890. current
811. thus	831. crowd	851. thick	871. stream	891. park
812. won't	832. poem	852. blood	872. planets	892. sell
813. cook	833. enjoy	853. lie	873. rhythm	893. shoulder
814. bones	834. elements	854. spot	874. eight	894. industry
815. tail	835. indicate	855. bell	875. science	895. wash
816. board	836. except	856. fun	876. major	896. block
817. modern	837. expect	857. loud	877. observe	897. spread
818 compound	838. flat	858. consider	878. tube	898. cattle
819. mine	839. seven	859. suggested	879. necessary	899. wife
820. wasn't	840. interesting	860. thin	880. weight	900. Sharp

901. company	921. France	941. shoes	961. workers	981. rope
902. radio	922. repeated	942. actually	962. Washington	982. cotton
903. we'll	923. column	943. nose	963. Greek	983. apple
904. action	924. western	944. afraid	964. women	984. details
905. capital	925. church	945. dead	965. bought	985. entire
906. factories	926. sister	946. sugar	966. led	986. corn
907. settled	927. oxygen	947.adjective	967. march	987substances
908. yellow	928. plural	948. fig	968. northern	988. smell
909. isn't	929. various	949. office	969. create	989. tools
910. southern	930. agreed	950. huge	970. British	990conditions
911. truck	931. opposite	951. gun	971. difficult	991. cows
912. fair	932. wrong	952. similar	972. match	992. track
913. printed	933. chart	953. death	973. win	993. arrived
914. wouldn't	934. prepared	954. score	974. doesn't	994. located
915. ahead	935. pretty	955. forward	975. steel	995. sir
916. chance	936. solution	956. stretched	976. total	996. seat
917. born	937. fresh	957. experience	977. deal	997. division
918. level	938. shop	958. rose	978. determine	998. effect
919. triangle	939. suffix	959. allow	979. evening	999. underline
920.molecules	940. especially	960. fear	980. nor	1000. View

Dolch Word List – Alphabetical

Pre-primer	*Primer*	*First*	*Second*	*Third*
a	all	after	always	about
and	am	again	around	better
away	are	an	because	bring
big	at	any	been	carry
blue	ate	as	before	clean
can	be	ask	best	cut
come	black	by	both	done
down	brown	could	buy	draw
find	but	every	call	drink
for	came	fly	cold	eight
funny	did	from	does	fall
go	do	give	don't	far
help	eat	going	fast	full
here	four	had	first	got
I	get	has	five	grow
in	good	her	found	hold
is	have	him	gave	hot
it	he	his	goes	hurt
jump	into	how	green	if
little	like	just	its	keep
look	must	know	made	kind
make	new	let	many	laugh
me	no	live	off	light
my	now	may	or	long
not	on	of	pull	much
one	our	old	read	myself
play	out	once	right	never
red	please	open	sing	only
run	pretty	over	sit	own
said	ran	put	sleep	pick
see	ride	round	tell	seven
the	saw	some	their	shall
three	say	stop	these	show
to	she	take	those	six
two	so	thank	upon	small
up	soon	them	us	start
we	that	then	use	ten
where	there	think	very	today
yellow	they	walk	wash	together

128

Pre-primer	Primer	First	Second	Third
you	this	were	which	try
	too	when	why	warm
	under		wish	
	want		work	
	was		would	
	well		write	
	went		your	
	what			
	white			
	who			
	will			
	with			
	yes			

Charts for Estimating Fluency

Assessing Reading Fluency – Timothy V. Rasinski, Ph.D., www.prel.org/products.re_/assessing-fluency.htm

Calculating Reading Fluency Document – www.buildingrti.utexas.org/PDF/Calculating_Fluency.pdf

Oral Reading Fluency Norms: Valuable Assessment Tool for Reading Teachers; Jan Hasbrouck and Gerald A. Tindal www.nclack.k12.or.us.cms.lib6.OR01000992/centricity/Do or www.k12.or.us

Finding Book Levels

www.Scholastic.com/bookwizard/   Type in name of book and you will receive: a summary of the book; information about the author; interest level of book; grade level of book; lexile measure; DRA level; Guided Reading Level.

Google Search for: Smog Readability Formula

Google Search for: Fry's Readability Graph

Google Search for Reading Level. For example, if you were reading, *Dog at the Door,* by Ben M. Baglio, you could open Google search and enter, "reading level for Dog at the Door". The search would return, "grade level equivalent 4.5". The back of the book has RL4, meaning "reading level fourth grade." This book is approximately at the level of a beginning to middle fourth grade level. Remember, this is not an age level. Any age could be at a fourth grade reading level depending on the child's abilities.

Many books will give an estimated reading level on the back of the book. For example, RL6 means "Reading Level Sixth Grade". This was found on the back cover, bottom left corner, under the price. The location will vary but many children's books label this level.

Reading Programs Based on Orton-Gillingham Methodology

Reading Blocks: A Step by Step Method to Teach Reading
Alphabetic Phonics
The Association Method
The Herman Approach
Lindamood-Bell
Montessori and Sequential English Education Approach
Academy of Orton-Gillingham Practitioners and Educators
Project Read
The Slingerland Multisensory Approach
The Spaulding Method
Wilson

Computer Games for Phonics and Reading

Check the compatibility of the program offered with your current computer software. Some of the older programs will not run on the newer computers. I have heard of people downloading a patch to convert the older program to the new software but this is out of my realm of experience. Just make sure you check before you buy.

Ohio Distinctive Software - www.ohio-distinctive.com. This company has many programs which are reasonably priced. A couple of the reading programs are: Woobies World of Phonics, Reader Rabbit: I Can Read with Phonics, Rock and Learn: Phonics and Reading.

The Learning Company – www.kidsclick.com. A few of the programs offered are: Jumpstart Phonics, Reading Blaster, Clifford Phonics, Arthur's First Grade, Arthur's Reading Games, and Clifford Reading.

Click and Read Phonics – www.clicknkids.com. This company offers a phonics program as well as a combination phonics and spelling program.

Reading Blaster and Word Munchers Deluxe can both be found on Amazon.

Multisensory Activities for Teaching Reading

An activity can be considered multisensory when more than one sense is used to complete a task. For example, tracing a letter on sandpaper while saying the sound aloud is a multisensory activity. This double action simultaneously activates more than one pathway in the neural systems of the brain, which helps the child to remember the targeted task. You want to build a strong pathway in the brain for the necessary phonological information for reading. This is done with explicit instruction and repeated practice. Picture the brain like an open field. You travel through that field every day for a shortcut. Eventually, there is a pathway worn into the grass from taking that shortcut. We want to develop these pathways in the brain which are necessary for reading effectively. Good readers already have these pathways but struggling readers can develop these pathways with the appropriate instruction. The following list contains several multisensory activities.

- Pour a layer of sand on a tray or cookie sheet. The sand should be a contrasting color to the bottom of the tray. The child writes the targeted letter while saying the sound aloud. The child sees the color contrast, feels the coarseness of the sand and the outline of the letter, and hears the voice making the sound as well as feels the movements in the mouth making the sound.
- First, show a letter and say the sound. Then have the child air write the letter using the whole arm while saying the sound. The child's eyes should be closed and the child is instructed to visualize the letter she is making on a particular colored board and a particular color letter. For example, black board and red letter. Now you have large muscle movement, hearing the sound, visualizing the colored letter.
- Write each letter on a colored square of tagboard. Copy over the letter with a bubble layer of glue and sprinkle sand over the glue. When this is dry, you can use the letters for tracing over while saying the sound. The child feels the texture, sees the color, hears the sound. You can also buy fat plastic letters that have a bumpy texture on the top. These are great for feeling the formation of letter while at the same time as saying the sound of the letter.
- Have the child use his finger to write the letter on his thigh or upper arm while saying the sound. The child has muscle movement of writing the letter, hears the sound, and feels the letter being formed on his thigh or upper arm. I also used my finger to trace the letter on my daughter's back and she had to guess the letter and then say the sound. The child feels the formation of the letter and has to visualize the letter and then retrieve the name and sound. This is more difficult and should be used on letters already practiced.
- Make letters out of clay. Then make words out of clay. Form the letter and then trace and say the sound.
- The child can use a stick or pencil to tap each sound she hears in a word. This helps the child to segment the word into sounds and to realize that each sound has its own tap.

- Have the child use her fingers to count out each sound in a word. Each sound gets one finger. This is very helpful when sounding out unknown words later on. We "count" the sounds aloud.
- Have the child take one large step for every sound in a word. "March" out the sounds.
- Use colored blocks to break a word into sounds. One color for each sound heard. Have the child move each block towards him for each sound in the word. When all the sounds are brought down and sounded he then reads the word. You can also use a colored tagboard with one, two, and three squares drawn. The word cat would be formed by putting a different colored block into each of the three squares. This uses muscle movement, visual activation, and sound. The squares also helps the child understand that the sounds in the word are separate.
- Throwing alphabet dice to make words. Use the squares again to form one, two, and three letter words.
- Use letter tiles to form words. Again, use the square boxes. Place one tile into one box. The letter tiles are also great for making and changing words. For example, start with four consonant letter tiles and one vowel letter tile, (p,t,s,c,a.) Make "cat" with the tiles. Child pulls each letter down and places in a box. Then change "cat" to "pat". Child has to decide which sound is different, move the changed letter up, and move the new letter down. Then have him count the three new sounds in the word using his fingers or tapping a pencil.
- Use a dry erase board or chalkboard to write letters and words. Use different colored markers.
- Make little paper books out of the sounds he knows first. Then make books out of the words he knows. Then make books out of the sentences he can read. Finally make books out of stories that he makes up using all the words he has practiced. These can be used for practicing his skills.
- Use colorful magnetic letter tiles on the refrigerator. Start with practicing sounds and then with making words. Write the letters you are practicing on colored cardboard and place on the wall around the child's bed. Use a pointer stick to practice before bed.
- Write sight words on colored paper or cardboard. Cut out and put on the walls around the child's bed. Use a pointer stick to search for the word by the beginning sound, or a rhyming word, or a similar middle or ending sound. Use these words to practice any skill needed.
- Always have tons of books to read at many different reading levels and interest levels. Have pens, markers, crayons, journals, and paper for writing and reading activities.
- Some children benefit by using the Irlen colored overlays. These are plastic overlays that can be placed over the page of a book. There are several different colors and usually a child prefers one color over the others. Some children experience success with these overlays and it is definitely worth mentioning.
- I always try to incorporate a variety of color into the reading lesson. Color provides for choices for the child which gives the child an opportunity to experience some control over the lesson. Color also stimulates areas in the brain and the more good stimulation, the better.

John McCarthy's Ode to His Children

Thinking

If you think you are beaten, you are
If you think you dare not, you don't,
If you like to win, but you think you can't
It is almost certain you won't.

If you think you'll lose, you're lost
For out of the world we find,
Success begins with a fellow's will
It's all in the state of mind.

If you think you are outclassed, you are
You've got to think high to rise,
You've got to be sure of yourself before
You can ever win a prize.

Life's battles don't always go
To the stronger or faster man,
But sooner or later the man who wins
Is the man WHO THINKS HE CAN

Walter D. Wintle

Reminders

Visit my website for more information and free downloads on the learning to read process. Sample videos are also available on how to effectively teach reading using *Reading Blocks: A Step by Step Method to Teach Reading*.

www.TheReadingTutor.org

Visit Gabriel Press for additional books and programs developed with the purpose of guiding each individual to a realization of his full potential.

www.GabrielPressUSA.com